HOTSPOTS
GOA

Written by Debbie Stowe
Original photography by Vasile Szakacs
Front cover photography © Thomas Cook
Series design based on an original concept by Studio 183 Limited

Produced by Cambridge Publishing Management Limited
Project Editor: Penny Isaac
Layout: Donna Pedley
Maps: PCGraphics

Published by Thomas Cook Publishing
A division of Thomas Cook Tour Operations Limited
Company Registration No. 1450464 England
PO Box 227, Coningsby Road
Peterborough PE3 8SB, United Kingdom
email: books@thomascook.com
www.thomascookpublishing.com
+ 44 (0) 1733 416477

ISBN: 978-1-84157-828-6

First edition © 2007 Thomas Cook Publishing
Text © 2007 Thomas Cook Publishing
Maps © 2007 Thomas Cook Publishing
Project Editor: Diane Ashmore
Production/DTP: Steven Collins

Printed and bound in Spain by GraphyCems

CONTENTS

INTRODUCTION 5
Getting to know Goa 8
The best of Goa 10
Symbols key 12

RESORTS 13
Arambol...14
Vagator 20
Anjuna...25
Baga 31
Calangute...37
Candolim 44
Sinquerim...48
Panaji...53
Colva 61
Benaulim 66
Palolem...70

EXCURSIONS 75
Bardez taluka 76
Fort Aguada 78
Dr Salim Ali Bird Sanctuary........81
Old Goa...83
Ponda...87
Margao...91

LIFESTYLE 95
Food & drink 96
Menu decoder 101
Shopping 104
Children 107
Sports & activities 109
Festivals & events.........................111

PRACTICAL INFORMATION...113
Preparing to go..............................114
During your stay 118

INDEX 125

MAPS
Goa 6
Anjuna..24
Baga 30
Calangute 36
Panaji...52
Colva...60
Margao..90

WHAT'S IN YOUR GUIDEBOOK?

Independent authors Impartial up-to-date information from our travel experts who meticulously source local knowledge.

Experience Thomas Cook's 165 years in the travel industry and guidebook publishing enriches every word with expertise you can trust.

Travel know-how Contributions by thousands of staff around the globe, each one living and breathing travel.

Editors Travel-publishing professionals, pulling everything together to craft a perfect blend of words, pictures, maps and design.

You, the traveller We deliver a practical, no-nonsense approach to information, geared to how you really use it.

INTRODUCTION
Getting to know Goa

Getting to know Goa

When you're travelling in Goa, it's sometimes easy to forget that it's just a tiny part of a very big country. The state's sense of identity is so strong that it feels like a nation in its own right, and the area is so lacking in the deprivations and hassles that can occur elsewhere in India that seasoned travellers often refer to it as 'India for beginners'. Its coastline of over 100 km (62 miles) – the majority of it consisting of golden beaches of a perfection that is rarely encountered outside holiday brochures – is supplemented by a few sites well worth venturing inland for. Goa's decent road and transport network makes it an easy place to get around, whether you choose to do so on the lively local buses that will set you back a few pence, in the luxury of a chauffeur-driven car, or – one of the most popular options – by motorbike.

Goa has all the cultural colour of India: if you're after temples, mysticism and Ayurveda, you won't have to look far. But the state also betrays influences from further afield: beautiful churches and villas remain one of the more positive legacies of around 450 years of Portuguese rule. Perhaps the most vibrant subculture in the state grew up through the free spirits who started arriving in the 1960s, when Goa was co-opted into the hippie trail. In northern resorts such as Arambol and Anjuna, the trail lives on in the hippie stalls, dreadlocks, Bob Marley memorabilia, trance music and a laidback vibe.

But there's plenty for more active types too. Calangute and Baga have become package hotspots and, with their pristine sands, numerous water sports and pulsating nightlife, it is obvious why. Inland, the administrative capital Panaji also offers a range of options after the sun goes down, with the thumping party boats that cruise up and down the river being among the most popular. Away from the buzz and nightlife are small havens of solitude and relaxation, where you can often have the beach and the sea almost to yourself, and catch a romantic sunset for two. If you get sand fatigue, Goa's backdrop of museums, places of worship, historical sites, animal sanctuaries and bird-watching areas means that it's impossible to get bored.

Factor in the often unbelievably cheap prices, welcoming Goans and an abundance of fantastic food – in particular fresh fruit and fish – and you'll start to understand why many of the holidaymakers who found their way to Goa never found their way back again.

△ Discover the colour and culture of a world apart

THE BEST OF GOA

Far more than just a beach resort, Goa has myriad delights to entertain you, from the mystic to the hedonistic. Whether you yearn for the serenity of meditation and massage, or the hair-raising thrills of jet-skiing and parasailing, everything you could ask of a beach holiday is on tap here – and all at an affordable price.

TOP 10 ATTRACTIONS

- **Ayurveda, yoga and meditation at Arambol** Whether you're a dedicated yogic or just fancy spoiling yourself with a relaxing massage, there are plenty of places willing to pummel, stretch or entrance you (see page 16).

- **Markets** Visit the vivid markets, such as the one at Calangute, which bring together local entrepreneurs, Western exiles and bargain-hunting tourists in a bustle of colour and noise (see page 39).

- **Learn to dive** Discover the amazing marine life around the Goan shore and explore ancient shipwrecks (see page 33).

- **The beach at Palolem** You know those wet weekday mornings back home when you're dreaming of the picture-perfect getaway? The place you're imagining is Palolem (see page 70).

- **Hippie scene in Anjuna** From its bustling market to the Bob Marley songs emanating from its beach bars, Anjuna is hippie-ville (see page 25).

- **Cocktails on the beach** Take refuge from the sun's heat with a White Russian or Sex on the Beach. Teetotallers can join in with a 'mocktail' (see page 23).

- **Portuguese architecture in Panaji** One of Goa's cultural highlights, the capital Panaji showcases the Portuguese architectural legacy at its best (see page 53).

- **Clubbing at Baga** When the sun goes down on another day at the beach, Baga's clubs are just warming up for another night of partying (see page 35).

- **Dining on fish** Fresh food fans can enjoy the ultimate treat: watching their dinner being hauled out of the sea, before eating it as waves lap the beach (see page 69).

- **Water sports at Sinquerim** In the sea or air; on a simple boat or speeding through waves at a hair-curling rate – the choice is yours (see pages 48–9).

🔽 *Fish sellers at Anjuna market*

SYMBOLS KEY
The following symbols are used throughout this book:

🄰 address 📞 telephone 📠 fax 🄴 email 🅦 website address
🕒 opening times ❶ important

The following symbols are used on the maps:

🛈	information office	O	city
📮	post office	O	large town
🛍	shopping	○	small town
🛧	airport	◼	poi (point of interest)
➕	hospital	=	motorway
🛡	police station	—	main road
🚌	bus station	—	minor road
🚆	railway station	—	railway
✝	church		
❶	numbers denote featured cafés, restaurants & evening venues		

RESTAURANT CATEGORIES
The symbol after the name of each restaurant listed in this guide indicates the cost of a typical three-course meal without drinks for one person:

£ up to 200 rupees ££ 200–400 rupees £££ over 400 rupees

▶ *Goa is a beach lover's dream*

RESORTS
Places under the sun

Arambol

Nestled right up near the northern tip of Goa, sociable Arambol has escaped the influx of package holidaymakers that has been seen by some of the more central beach resorts. Instead, it has been taken over by a different breed: hippies. Independent travellers, free spirits and anyone with dreadlocks will fit right in here; in fact it's hard for anyone not to feel at home in a place with such a sense of community. Restaurateurs are friendly and relaxed, there's plenty of communal entertainment like film nights, and dotted around are little notices advertising everything from music lessons to massage.

BEACHES

Arambol's beautiful beach has retained elements of the authentic India. Colourful fishing boats pepper the golden sand. To the right as you face out to sea is a rugged hill, with a few palms and cottages. Despite the resort's popularity among the backpacker and hippie crowd, there's always plenty of room on the beach, perhaps because of its relative remoteness. The long and wide expanse of sand holds plenty of eateries, so you'll never be stuck for a spot of lunch or a cooling cocktail. The lush trees dotted among the bars and restaurants mean that the resort feels less commercial than other locations.

You won't have any trouble finding a sunbed and umbrella. As in most of Goa, these are usually owned by the restaurants nearest to them and are typically free to use if you're eating or drinking at that establishment; otherwise you'll be expected to pay a small charge.

If you fancy a dip, be warned that at times the sea can be fairly rough, so weak swimmers may be better off in one of the resort's freshwater lakes.

THINGS TO SEE & DO

Watersports

Fans of peace and quiet will be pleased to hear that Arambol has escaped the noisier, engine-propelled watersports, but adventurous types can do a spot of surfing and paragliding.

The **Surf Club and Shack**, something of a one-stop-shop for all your leisure needs, not only rents out watersports equipment and offers basic tuition, but also shows films on Monday, hosts an open-mic music night with buffet on Tuesday, offers a DJ on Wednesday and live music again – this time by the professionals – on Friday. Other entertainments run the gamut from massage to pool and board games.

🅐 60 m (200 ft) off the south end of Arambol Beach 🅣 9850554006
🅔 flyinfishbarbados@hotmail.com

🔺 *Sand, surf and eating shacks at Arambol*

Kite Surf Goa is a German-run outfit that hires out equipment and offers surfing courses.

ⓐ Ask at the Surf Club ❶ 9822867570

Yoga and meditation

Hippie hub Arambol offers seemingly unlimited ways to treat yourself to a bit of mysticism. Check the notice boards for new offers. Many outfits spend half the year in Goa and the rest in Dharamsala in north India.

Himalayan Iyengar Yoga Centre One of the most established yoga operators in the area. Five-day courses start every Friday at 08.30. Booking can be done in person every Tuesday at 14.00 from the centre itself.

ⓐ Between Arambol and Mandrem beaches: look for signs ❶ 01892 221312
ⓔ info@hiyogacentre.com ⓦ www.hiyogacentre.com ❶ Mid-Nov–Apr

Panda Tai Chi Meditation and Tai Chi are two of the workshops on offer.
ⓐ Tai Chi Garden next to Priya guesthouse, Coconut Grove and the beach by Full Moon ❶ No phone ⓔ pandataichi@yahoo.com
ⓦ www.pandataichi.net ❶ Nov–mid-Mar

Universal Yoga Daily classes and courses start at 09.00 (except Sunday), while Hatha yoga is from 16.00–18.00.
ⓐ Opposite Narayan Temple ❶ 9418291929 ⓦ www.vijaypoweryoga.com
❶ Mon–Sat, closed Sun

TAKING A BREAK

Bars & cafés

Arambol essentially consists of one main road leading to the beach, where the majority of eating and drinking options are concentrated. This makes getting lost or failing to find your intended venue practically impossible.

Café Mazal £ Making a pleasant – and nutritional – change from the stereotypical beach shack, the friendly Café Mazal provides homemade Yemeni, Middle Eastern and Arabic health food in a laidback venue with straw mats and cheerful blue and yellow drapes. The fare on offer

includes falafel, raw salads, health drinks, couscous and soup, with some
daily specials. The tea bar has hot and cold herb and flower tea and
imported Turkish and Arabic coffee. Movies, jam sessions and concerts
are held in the Shakti garden. ⓐ Khalchawada ⓣ No phone
🕐 09.00–01.00 Mon–Sun

Cookie Wallah £ At the other end of the scale to Café Mazal, the Cookie
Wallah will bring you all manner of guilty indulgences – cakes, cookies,
apple pie or chocolate brownies – or a sandwich if you prefer, while you
relax on cushions or low comfy chairs. Very friendly and homely.
ⓐ Khalchawada, opposite Piya guesthouse ⓣ No phone
🕐 08.00–23.00 or 24.00

Happy Banana Juice Bar £ Fruit fans rejoice! This tiny shack offers juices,
shakes, lassis and healthy breakfasts like muesli. Choose from the whole
gamut of fruit including mango, papaya, pineapple and pomegranate.
Sensation seekers can try out adventurous combinations like the melon
and chocolate milkshake. The jolly slogan is: 'Smile a lot. It costs nothing.'
ⓐ Khalchawada ⓣ 9850945403 ⓔ happybanana@yahoo.com
🕐 08.00–23.00 Mon–Sun

Lamuela £ Friendly café and salad bar serving freshly made salads,
sandwiches, coffee, tea, pure juices, bagels, ice cream, shakes and
smoothies, all of which you can enjoy from a swinging seat. It has a small
shop, and also offers *reiki*, massage, reflexology, acupuncture, Ayurvedic
head and yoga massage, Thai massage and something called Tibetan
singing bowl therapy. A mystic tarot card reader is available on Sunday
and Monday. Other options include drum and self-defence lessons,
Tai Chi from 17.00 to 18.00 Monday to Friday, and rooftop Chi Gong lessons.
ⓐ 292 Khalchawada, around the corner from the church ⓣ 9822486314
ⓔ lamuella@gmail.com 🕐 08.30–23.00 Mon–Sun, mid-Aug–mid-May

Mamma Mia £ Lovers of Italy's coffee and cake culture can choose from
bread, pizza, focaccia, croissant, sandwiches, *pane e Nutella*, sweets,

mocha coffee, cappuccino and hot chocolate. ❸ Khalchawada
❸ 9850473468 ❹ 08.00–01.00 Tues–Sun, closed Mon

AFTER DARK

Restaurants

Dawat £ Good-humouredly billing itself as the 'budget restaurant for budget people', Dawat offers cheap eats against a background of mellow music.
❸ Khalchawada ❸ 9881463731, 9881284294 ❹ 08.00–23.00 Mon–Sun

Blue Sea Horse ££ Popular in large part due to a canny entertainment programme of three easy-watching films a day (think *Top Gun* and the like), at 18.00, 20.00 and 21.30, plus football, live music, a pool table and cocktails. As well as the usual breakfast, Indian, Chinese, tandoori and Italian options, Israeli and Portuguese food also features. ❸ At junction of beach and road ❸ 0832 6515232, 9225902344 ❹ 07.00–02.00 Mon–Sun

Double Dutch ££ Large, fun garden restaurant with trees creating separate sections for a touch of privacy, and a more informal dining area with big cushions to relax on. The Indonesian food gets good write-ups, as do the desserts, which include apple pie, cakes, cheesecake and cookies. Catch a sitar concert on Sunday morning, or check out what's going on in Arambol on the so-called 'bullshit info' board at the entrance, covered in adverts for music lessons, yoga and Ayurveda treatments. There's also a book swap. ❸ Beach Road ❸ 0832 6525973 ❹ doubledutchgoa@yahoo.co.uk ❹ 07.00–23.00 Mon–Sun

Fellini ££ Highly rated Italian restaurant with an outdoor clay oven from which delectable pizzas emerge after 18.30. Other options include beef, chicken and pasta dishes, or toast and sandwiches if you just fancy a snack. The relaxed staff and outdoor tables create a laidback vibe, and there's also a small jewellery shop. ❸ Beach Road ❹ 10.00–23.00 Mon, Tues, Thur–Sat, 18.30–23.00 Wed, 11.00–23.00 Sun, opens last week in Nov–May

Loekie Café ££ Another easy-going eatery with cushions and live music.
Jam sessions are held on Thursday and Sunday. The menu includes
continental, Italian, Chinese, Indian, English, tandoori, seafood and
cocktails. From 09.00 to 20.00 they also offer massages; to book one, call
🕿 9822037412. ⓐ Beach Road 🕿 0832 5629632, 9822149097
🕒 08.00–24.00 Mon–Sun

Morning Star ££ Unpretentious eatery, serving a typical beach-shack
menu of pizza, European standards, Italian favourites and seafood.
ⓐ Harmal Beach 🕿 9822486487 🕒 08.00–23.00 Mon–Sun

Sai Sagar bar and restaurant ££ Rumour has it that Raj, the friendly
owner of this place, has appeared on the BBC's *Food & Drink* programme.
The Indian food is recommended, and you can sometimes catch a film.
ⓐ Main Road 🕿 9881200969 🕒 07.00–23.00 or later Mon–Sun

🔺 *Colourful lanterns on sale in Arambol*

Vagator

Vagator is something of a contradiction. Its coastline is rugged, sometimes windswept, and made up of secluded inlets, as opposed to the straight, uninterrupted stretches of sand found elsewhere. While it can get busy with day-trippers, in the morning and late afternoon it is relatively unoccupied and the few groups there tend to be locals rather than tourists, giving it an authentic Indian feel. This also means that you're liable to be the subject of some staring if you're in your bikini. But the area's remoteness and peacefulness hide a secret: Vagator is one of Goa's top nightlife spots, home to several of the state's long-established party venues.

As well as committed clubbers, the small numbers of tourists make Vagator a good stop-off for anyone who prefers a less packaged atmosphere. The seclusion and privacy are also a big draw for couples, and the palm-strewn hill by the market overlooking the sea is one of the most romantic places in the state from which to watch the sun go down.

BEACHES

There are three beaches in the area: from north to south, Vagator, Little Vagator and Ozran. The main one is Vagator, but Little Vagator is also popular with visitors because of the image of the Hindu god Shiva carved into the rocks. As with many Goan resorts, don't be surprised to find yourself sharing the beach with members of the local bovine community.

At the approach to the beach, by the car park, is a small market, where you can enjoy (or endure – they're not to everyone's taste) a freshly made sugar cane juice. There are a few tourist-oriented stalls, but you won't get the hard sell. From the car park, some rough-hewn steps lead down to the beach. Steep and irregular, these are difficult to negotiate and care is required. If you want to swim, it's better to stick to Vagator Beach, which is sometimes patrolled by a lifeguard and has a flag warning system in place; the rocky waters at Ozran make the current unpredictable.

The coastline here has undergone nothing like the commercialisation of the larger resorts. There is the odd place to eat on the beach, but by and large when you're looking out to sea there are cliffs rather than beach shacks behind you. Rocks on the beach and green-brown hills to the right add to the naturalistic, undeveloped feel. Your time here is unlikely to be disturbed by the roar of jet-ski engines: sport in Vagator usually means nothing more energetic than Frisbee or volleyball.

TAKING A BREAK

Bars & cafés
Bean Me Up £ Lively and popular organic and veggie restaurant, where pizzas, pastas, wraps and juices are consumed by a casual crowd in the courtyard. Thursday night is film night, live music or dance is usually on Sunday and there are also Ayurveda treatments available. Kids get mattresses, colouring books and cartoons on the TV. ❸ 1639/2 Deul

🔺 *The natural vibe of Vagator*

Vaddo ☎ 0832 2273479 ⊜ beanmeup@usa.net ⏱ 12.00–16.00,
19.00–23.00 Sun–Fri ⓘ Credit cards accepted

Shri Mahalaxmi £ An appropriately no-frills restaurant for the rugged,
un-touristy Vagator, Shri Mahalaxmi enjoys a near monopoly on the
beach. A big hall with a well-stocked bar and a TV, they warn you of a
25-minute wait for your food, but the service is cheerful and helpful.
➋ Beachfront, down steps and to right ☎ 0832 6510161 ⏱ 09.00–23.00 or
24.00 Mon–Sun

AFTER DARK

Restaurants
Garden Villa £ Pleasant restaurant with a peaceful garden and film
nights. The quality food, particularly the Chinese and continental dishes,
attracts many repeat customers. ➋ Vagator Beach Road ☎ 0832 5629454,
9822104780 ⊜ garden@goatelecom.com ⏱ 08.00–23.00 Mon–Sun

Bamboo Palace ££ The bamboo décor and comfy chairs lend this place a
mellow vibe, as does the friendly staff. Choose from steaks, pizza, pasta,
salads, tandoori and curry, washed down with a juice or cocktail from the bar.
➋ Vagator Beach Road ☎ 0832 2273071, 9326121699 ⏱ 11.00–23.00 Mon–Sun

Le Bluebird ££ This French-run restaurant enjoys a great reputation,
particularly for its seafood. Veggies will also enjoy the wide range of
meat-free options. The imported wine and champagne is another big
draw. ➋ Close to Little Vagator Beach ☎ 0832 2273695 ⏱ 09.30–14.00,
19.00–23.00 Mon–Sun

Mango Tree ££ The Chinese food at this open-air eatery gets a thumbs-
up, and there's also Thai, Italian and Mexican to choose from. The film,
shown every night at 19.30, is popular, but it's not the place to pitch up at
if you're starving as the service can be slow. ➋ Opposite the Mapusa bus
stand ☎ 0832 3094464 ⏱ 09.00–23.00 Mon–Sun, open all year

Willy's ££ The staff and food both get good reviews here, which has the usual pizzas, sandwiches, continental, Indian, Chinese, tandoori, Goan and Israeli fare. Follow it with ice cream and cocktails. ➍ Vagator Beach Road ❶ 0832 2273566, 9422057574 ❺ willy100@hotmail.com ❻ 08.30–00.30 Mon–Sun

⬥ Watch the sun go down as you sip a cocktail

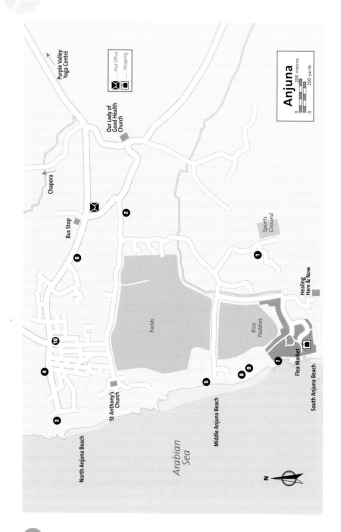

Anjuna

0 ——— 200 metres
0 ——— 200 yards

Post Office
Shopping

Purple Valley
Yoga Centre

Chapora

Bus Stop

Our Lady of
Good Health
Church

Sports
Ground

Healing
Here & Now

Fields

Rice
Paddies

St Anthony's
Church

Flea Market

North Anjuna Beach

Middle Anjuna Beach

South Anjuna Beach

Arabian
Sea

N

Anjuna

Anjuna will appeal to anyone who finds its moniker, 'freak capital of the world', a good thing, and vies with Arambol, further up the coast, for the title of Goa's top hippie resort. It's more spread out than Arambol and as a result lacks some of the community feel, but the renowned Wednesday flea market floods the town with atmosphere and character. Anjuna was once famous for trance parties; now the authorities are clamping down on noise pollution, and such gatherings are becoming harder to find. But you can still have a great night out here, particularly on market day, which draws in visitors from all around. Taxi drivers are usually the best information sources on parties.

BEACHES

Even on market day, the beach at Anjuna remains fairly free of crowds. It's a wide, flat expanse of sand, dotted with a few beach shacks with a smattering of tables on the sand and market stalls, but is nowhere near as cluttered as the more package-oriented resorts further south. The beach is wide and flat with tall palms, and the unusual black rock formation is perfectly in keeping with the alternative feel of the resort. You don't get as many swimmers as elsewhere, but the water is relatively safe. Sunbeds are also available.

Primarily a market town, Anjuna does attract more than its fair share of seasoned hawkers, and these spill over onto the beach. They can be fairly determined, but if your 'noes' are firm enough they should leave you alone. More welcome beach entrepreneurs are the jugglers and fire-eaters who sometimes strut their stuff in the early evening.

THINGS TO SEE & DO

Flea Market

One of Goa's top tourist draws, the huge Anjuna market is an overwhelming fusion of all the colour, noise and commerce of Goa. If you don't find something you want to buy from the shoes, clothes, jewellery, music, pashminas, shawls, cushion covers, CDs, spices, bric-à-brac, hookah pipes, sunglasses and cigarettes on offer, you must be very hard to please. Part of the attraction is that the market attracts many vibrant individuals, from expat hippies to Goan matriarchs and Indian men with piercings that seem to defy science. Not everyone exudes a positive presence, though: some of the traders and beggars can be persistent to the point of annoying. If it's getting tiresome, head for the covered jewellery market run by Tibetan vendors, where you'll get less of the hard sell. You can also appease your conscience at the section for project and charity appeals. There are several cafés, most quite far from the entrance, plus ice-cream *wallahs* doing the rounds.

ⓐ Market Road, at southern end of beach ⓒ 08.00–17.00 Wed, Oct–Mar or Apr

△ *Surf and sailpower at Anjuna*

Yoga

Healing Here & Now Yoga and healing treatments.
ⓐ Behind Xavier's restaurant ❶ 0832 2268158, 9822488791
ⓔ info@healinghereandnow.com ⓦ www.healinghereandnow.com

Purple Valley Yoga Centre Choose from various yoga and meditation courses with international instructors. The managers are also introducing Ayurvedic and beauty treatments.
ⓐ 142 Bairo Alto, Assagao, between Anjuna and Mapusa ❶ 0832 2268364
ⓔ theresa_appleby@hotmail.com ⓦ www.yogagoa.com 🕒 09.00–18.00, Nov–Apr

TAKING A BREAK

Bars & cafés

German Bakery £ ❶ This is the original bakery that has spawned imitators all over Goa. Its juices, sweets and coffee are particularly

🔺 *Anjuna market is a big attraction*

recommended, and it also serves main courses. ➋ Behind Flea Market
🛈 No phone 🕒 08.30–23.00 Mon–Sun

Mermaids Café & Boutique £ ➋   Delightfully serene café-cum-
boutique selling lemonade, coffee and sandwiches, as well as high-end
hippie clothes. ➌ 973 Montierro Vaddo, opposite football ground
🛈 9822197015, 9822197380 🕒 09.00–18.00 Mon–Fri, 09.00–16.00 Sat,
closed Sun

Zoori's £ ➌   The comfy cushions and good view recommend Zoori's,
which does breakfasts, salads and light meals like burgers.
➌ 652 St Anthony Praise, near the bus stand 🛈 0832 2273476,
9822586623 🖂 hornykarma@hotmail.com 🕒 10.00–01.00 Mon–Sun

AFTER DARK

Restaurants
Biryani Palace £ ➍   A lantern-bedecked and fairy-lit marquee with a
big model snake in the middle, Biryani Palace makes an atmospheric

🔺 *Enjoy a rich range of spices in Goan fare*

venue to enjoy seafood, kebabs, biryanis and other Indian fare. ⓐ Anjuna Beach Road ⓣ 9326124699, 9850463631 ⓛ 11.00–24.00 Mon–Sun

Antonio's Café ££ ❺ Typically mellow beachfront choice with comfy seats overlooking the sea and Bob Marley on the CD player. ⓐ Anjuna Beach ⓣ 9822032396 ⓛ 08.00–23.00 Mon–Sun

Blue Tao ££ ❻ Highly rated health-food restaurant serving vegetarian and organic dishes with an emphasis on Italian and Indian cuisine. There's also occasional live music. The Aroma shop sells new-age therapeutic oils, perfumes and gifts. ⓐ Anjuna Beach Road, 300 m (980 ft) west of post office ⓣ 0832 2273977, 9850419782 ⓔ martaceriani@yahoo.com ⓛ 09.30–23.00 Mon–Sun

Café Looda ££ ❼ Right by the flea market, Café Looda has a great atmosphere on Wednesday, when it hosts a live band. There's also sitar and relaxing music from 18.00 on Sundays. ⓐ On the beach right by the flea market ⓣ 9822142272, 9850792571 ⓛ 09.00–23.00 Mon–Sun

Janet and John's Multicuisine Restaurant ££ ❽ Friendly place whose big night is Monday, when there's a 35-dish seafood buffet. ⓐ Anjuna Beach, 300 m (980 ft) from flea market ⓣ 9822125929 ⓛ 08.00–24.00 Mon–Sun

Lilliput ££ ❾ Arranged with the seats facing out to sea as if gazing towards a theatre stage, this charming bar and restaurant enjoys mellow music and a pool table. ⓐ Govenkar Vaddo, Anjuna Beach ⓣ 0832 2274648, 9822137767 ⓛ 08.00–24.00 Mon–Sun

Starco ££ ❿ Loud and lively bar and restaurant serving Indian and continental food. Sit outside if you can to enjoy the fairy lights. ⓐ At the Starco junction ⓣ No phone ⓛ 08.30–24.00 Mon–Sun

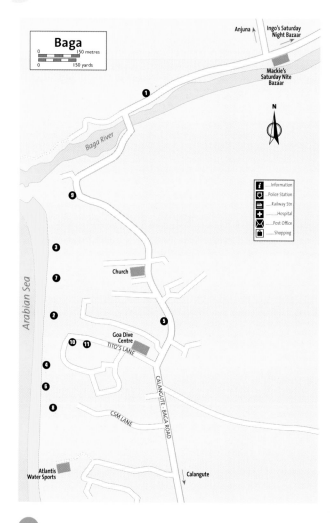

Baga

0 — 150 metres
0 — 150 yards

Anjuna

Ingo's Saturday Night Bazaar

Mackie's Saturday Nite Bazaar

Baga River

N

1

9

i .... Information
.... Police Station
.... Railway Stn
.... Hospital
.... Post Office
.... Shopping

3

7

Church

2

5

10 11

Goa Dive Centre

TITO'S LANE

4

6

8

CALANGUTE-BAGA ROAD

CSM LANE

Arabian Sea

Atlantis Water Sports

Calangute

Baga

Probably Goa's nightlife capital, Baga is home to the big-name clubs that attract the party set, and its after-dark scene is considered more sophisticated than nearby Calangute's. Here nights are for partying hard; days are for recovering and going for it again, this time on jet-skis or parasailing. One of the main package-tour hubs, the resort is full of Europeans flown in by tour companies, so attracts groups of friends out to socialise and have fun with other holidaymakers. Because of the youthful vibe, there are a lot of watersports options, with operators patrolling the beach looking for customers. As well as the extreme stuff, you also have the more sedate options of crocodile- and dolphin-spotting on the Mandovi River: the crocs nestle among the tree-lined river banks and the dolphins cavort where the river meets the sea.

As well as the sea there is the Baga River, which flows inland north of the beach and is a good option for weaker swimmers who find the sea waves off-putting.

BEACHES

Crescent-shaped Baga beach is slightly less crowded and developed than its immediate neighbour, Calangute. At low tide the beach is wide and gently sloping, but at high tide it does get fairly narrow. You shouldn't have trouble in finding a sunbed – as usual these are free if you're eating in the restaurant that owns them, otherwise a charge of around 50 rupees is normal.

The sea is calmer than at Calangute, so relatively safe for swimming, but serious surfers will have to go elsewhere for their waves. Along with the watersports *wallahs*, masseurs also wander the beach selling their services. But there's no need to do anything on Baga Beach: with the paddy fields behind you, verdant cliffs to your left and waves crashing poetically off the rocks, it's enough simply to relax and take in the scenery.

◯ Beautiful Baga

THINGS TO SEE & DO

Markets

Ingo's Saturday Night Bazaar The larger of the two Baga markets, Ingo's has clothes, crafts and jewellery along with live music and fire-twirling.
ⓐ Arpora, halfway between Baga and Anjuna ⓘ 16.30–24.00 Sat, Nov–Mar

Mackie's Saturday Nite Bazaar Smaller and calmer than its rival, this is within walking distance of Baga.
ⓐ Near Mahrinha Dourado, near Baga Creek ⓘ 9881772990
ⓘ 18.00–24.00 Sat, Nov–Mar

Watersports

Atlantis Water Sports Offers scuba diving, jet-skiing, parasailing and windsurfing at negotiable prices.
ⓐ Where Vila Goesa Road meets the beach ⓘ 0832 3092909, 9890047272

Goa Dive Centre With another outlet in Candolim, the Goa Dive Centre offers PADI scuba-diving courses and snorkelling.
ⓐ Tito's Lane ⓘ 9822157094 ⓘ 16.00–21.00

TAKING A BREAK

Lila Café £ ❶ Salads, rolls and omelettes are on offer at this popular German-run bakery and café, alongside cakes and desserts.
ⓐ Near Baga River ⓘ 0832 2279843 ⓔ lilacafe@sify.com
ⓦ www.lilacafegoa.com ⓘ 09.00–18.00 Wed–Mon, closed Tues

AFTER DARK

Restaurants

Le Marin beach shack £ ❷ One of many similar options on Baga beach, this is a good place for couples with two-seater tables facing out to the sea. The service is efficient, and there's often sport showing on the TV. ❷ Near Tito's, Sauntavaddo ✆ 9822877718, 9822382820 🕐 07.00–03.00 (sometimes 24 hours) Mon–Sun

Andrew's ££ ❸   Quiet, calm and cool, this beach shack has a thatched roof, swing seats, plants and a pool table. ❷ 7/62 Sauntavaddo ✆ 9822151678 🕐 07.30–last customer Mon–Sun

Antonio's ££ ❹   One of the first shacks to set up on the beach, affable Antonio's has a nice atmosphere, great food and friendly staff. It's a quiet place, where you can relax among the plants and peruse the magazine collection. There's a brightly painted mural and the obligatory Bob Marley artwork. Sunday night's seafood barbecue serves up kingfish, shark, tuna and rockfish fillet. ❷ Cobravaddo, Baga Road ✆ 0832 2282108, 0832 2277166, 9860027173 🕐 09.00–23.30 or 24.00 Mon–Sun

Casa Portuguesa ££ ❺   Housed in an exquisite Goan-Portuguese manor replete with antiques and a stylish terrace, the cuisine includes indulgent specials such as roast wild boar. ❷ On the left hand side of Baga Road, 200 m (660 ft) past the Hotel Ronil ✆ 0832 2277024 🕐 19.00–23.00 Tues–Sun, closed Mon, Nov–Apr

TGI Friday ££ ❻   This shack is as relaxed and lively as the restaurant chain whose name it is cheekily borrowing. ❷ Near Tito's, to the left of Antonio's facing the sea ✆ 9822139660 🕐 08.00–24.00 (or until last customer leaves) Mon–Sun

Zanzibar ££ ❼   With leather seats and an upmarket ambience, this is a more sophisticated alternative than most of its competitors. You can also pick up a pair of flip-flops here. ❷ Down Tito's Lane and to right, on beach by volleyball net ✆ 9823274707 🕐 09.00–01.30 or 02.00 Mon–Sun

Bars & clubs

Bosco's ££ **8** Perennially popular restaurant-nightspot, with a barbecue on Tuesday and karaoke on Friday from 19.00. Happy hour runs from 17.00–19.00, with two-for-one cocktails. Ice cream and European wines, though not together, are two of the other attractions. Food is served until 23.30 by genial staff. **③** Near Colonia Santa Maria, Cobravaddo **①** 0832 2277862 **①** 08.00–01.00 Mon–Sun, Nov–May

Britto's ££ **9** Baga stalwart with highly rated seafood plus a range of Indian and continental choices, Britto's also has a reputation as a lively nightspot. Its popularity means at peak times it can take a while to get served – but you can enjoy the view while you wait. The cakes and pastries are top-notch as well. **③** Baga Beach **①** 0832 2277331 **①** 07.00–03.00 Mon–Sun

Café Mambo ££ **10** Affiliated to and just a few metres closer to the sea than Tito's, this beachfront venue is not quite as lively as its mother club, but is still one of the top nightspots in the area, playing host to big international DJs. Dinner is served from 19.00, and the disco starts at 22.00. **③** On beachfront, Tito's Lane **①** 0832 2279895 **①** 24 hours Mon–Sun **①** Admission charge for disco

Tito's £££ **11** Now over 35 years old, this legendary Baga nightclub has hosted Richard Gere and the cream of the Bollywood set among other beautiful people. The restaurant serves Goan cuisine, pizzas and homemade desserts, and there's also an outdoors pub. Entertainment runs the gamut from magicians to Goan folk dancing, while club nights include jungle, retro, karaoke and hip-hop, plus ladies' night. **③** Tito's Lane **①** 0832 2279895, 9822765002 **①** 0832 2279895 **④** webmaster@titosgoa.com **①** www.titosgoa.com **①** Disco from 22.00–02.00 Mon–Sun **①** Admission charge for men and couples

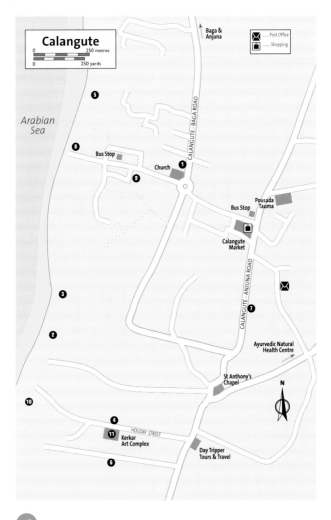

Calangute

0		250 metres
0		250 yards

Post Office
Shopping

Baga & Anjuna

Arabian Sea

CALANGUTE - BAGA ROAD

❺

❽ Bus Stop

❾ Church ❶

Bus Stop

Pousada Tauma

Calangute Market

CALANGUTE - ANJUNA ROAD

❼

❸

❷

Ayurvedic Natural Health Centre

St Anthony's Chapel

N

❿

❹ HOLIDAY STREET

⓫ Kerkar Art Complex

Day Tripper Tours & Travel

❻

Calangute

Calangute was the first Goan resort that foreigners homed in on. It has never looked back and is now the most popular and busiest holiday destination in the state. The name means land of the fisherman, but it's abundantly clear that it's tourism rather than fishing that is the town's main concern. It was the hippies who first happened upon the resort and got the tourism ball rolling, but Calangute is now decidedly mainstream: while you can still pick up hippie clothes, bags and knick-knacks from the stalls, the alternative travellers now go further north, to Arambol and Aranjuna. These days, Calangute is a veritable temple to tourism, with wall-to-wall beach shacks, top entertainment and eating options and Western-style shopping facilities. All of this attracts plenty of Indians as well as overseas visitors, all enjoying the holiday vibe.

The crowd consists of holidaymakers who prefer to have everything they could possibly need at their fingertips and don't want to work too hard to get it. With so many different ways to pass the time, from just messing about on the beach and playing a spot of volleyball to hair-raising watersports and teeming nightspots, there's something for everyone, which makes Calangute a good choice for family groups, or gangs of pals looking to party hard at night and sleep it off on the beach the next day.

Despite its package-'n'-party reputation, Calangute yields some surprisingly cultural treats. It's one of the best beach resorts in the state for art lovers, with several galleries of note, many of which also offer works for sale. Shopaholics will also have their appetites sated in the town, which has both posh designer boutiques and an Indian market.

BEACHES

The central and busiest area of the beach is at the end of the road leading to the roundabout, where a set of wide steps leads down to the sand. Here you'll find a selection of stalls and shops. Despite Calangute's popularity, it is possible to get away from the sunbathing masses. The beach is very wide, and there's space both in front of and behind the rows of sunbathers. While the main section is heaving with sunbeds and umbrellas, if you're prepared to walk a little way either north or south you'll come to less populated parts where you can find some privacy and

● *Peace is still possible in popular Calangute*

see some empty sand among the sun-seekers. Those wanting a more active time are also well catered for in Calangute, with watersports hawkers constantly strolling around the beach aiming to put tourists in boats, in the air or on jet-skis. There are also volleyball nets if you don't want your activity too strenuous, although in the Goan heat almost any activity can feel a bit much. Cooling off in the water is always tempting, and usually safe, but it can get rough, especially in the afternoon. Look out for a lifeguard.

THINGS TO SEE & DO

Ayurveda

Ayurvedic Natural Health Centre All sorts of yoga and Ayurvedic treatments, from one-off email consultations and two-and-a-half-hour taster programmes to six-week intensive yoga courses for all abilities. Helpful staff offer free guided tours, 10.30–17.30 Mon–Sat.

ⓐ Chogm Road, Saligao ⓣ 0832 2409036, 9422448973

ⓔ info@healthandayurveda.com ⓛ 10.00–20.30

Pousada Tauma If you're serious about your Ayurveda and have time to spare, this centre is also a boutique hotel that offers treatment and accommodation packages.

ⓐ Porba Vaddo ⓣ 0832 2279061/2/3 ⓕ 0832 2279064

ⓔ neville@pousada-tauma.com ⓦ www.pousada-tauma.com

ⓛ 07.30–22.30, Jan–Dec

Calangute Market

In a congested part of town, the market is another good opportunity to hone your haggling skills, whether you're after leather goods, clothes, jewellery souvenirs, metalwork or some food. Slightly further towards the beach, by the church, you can pick up Tibetan and Kashmiri textiles and handicrafts, and even further on there are sarongs, other beach essentials – and fortune-tellers. While you're there, pop into the eye-catching temple, open from 07.00–19.30.

Kerkar Art Complex

Hosting the sculptures and painting of the founder, famous Goan watercolourist Subodh Kerkar, plus other Indian artists. The site also has an open-air auditorium, which holds concerts of classical Indian music and dance on Tuesdays between 18.45 and 20.30 for 300 rupees.

ⓐ Gaurawaddo, South Calangute ⓣ 0832 2276017 ⓕ 0832 2276509
ⓔ subodhkerkar@satyam.net.in ⓦ www.subodhkerkar.com

Watersports & boat trips

Calangute and Baga are arguably the epicentre of Goa's watersports industry, with windsurfing, jet-skiing and parasailing just a few of the options. Calangute is also a good starting point for exploring further afield.

Day Tripper Tours and Travel offers the usual tours and boat trips within Goa plus trips over several days further afield to the Taj Mahal and Golden

◭ *Parasailing is one sporting option*

Triangle. ⓐ E1/79A Gaura Vaddo, near Kamat Complex ☎ 0832 2276726
ⓔ info@daytrippergoa.com 🕐 09.00–17.30 Mon–Sat, 09.00–12.30 Sun

TAKING A BREAK

Bars & cafés
Infantaria Pastry Shop £ ❶ Popular bakery whose pastries, cakes,
croissants and snacks are also available to take away. The notice board is
a great source of information on yoga and Ayurveda in the area.
ⓐ Umtawaddo ☎ 0832 2277421 🕐 08.00–20.00 Mon–Sun

Natural-ly £ ❷ Calm and quiet beach shack doing the usual food, with
a shop selling bags, clothes and jewellery. ⓐ On the beach ☎ 9823231458
🕐 08.00–22.00 or later Mon–Sun

AFTER DARK

Chasing Chengs ££ ❸ Relaxing hangout with cushions around the
tables and an extensive cocktail menu. On Thursday there's a barbecue
with a Brazilian dancer in attendance, while Saturday is firework night,
all from 21.00. ⓐ Beach shack no 7, to left of road ☎ 9960076435,
9881475746 🕐 10.00–24.00 Mon–Sun

Emma's Kitchen ££ ❹ Upmarket English place catering to Brits abroad,
who particularly enjoy the Sunday roast dinner. The black-and-white
colour scheme, complete with tablecloths, is as traditional as the menu.
There's a nice terrace, and the bar serves drinks and snacks.
ⓐ Holiday Street, opposite Kerkar Art Gallery ☎ 9890392073
ⓔ emmajgoa@yahoo.com 🕐 09.00–12.30, 19.00–24.00 Mon–Sun, Oct–Apr

Horizon ££ ❺ Serving mainly Chinese and Indian food – the prawn
biryani is particularly recommended. Live football is shown on the TV and
there's also a pool table. ⓐ Umtawaddo ☎ 9822183606, 9822484114
🕐 08.00–23.00 Mon–Sun

La Fenice & Coffee Garden ££ **6** Highly regarded Italian that imports many ingredients and offers real espressos and fresh pasta. It's on three levels and has a rooftop terrace. ⊙ Candolim-Calangute Road, Gaura Vaddo opposite Tarcar Ice Factory ⊙ 0832 2281182, 9890200840 ⊙ 09.00–24.00 Mon–Sun

Midaas Touch ££ **7** From the outside, this gaudy place resembles a water park. Inside it's bright and cheerful, with good-quality Goan, Chinese and continental food, sometimes accompanied by live music. The air-conditioned dining room offers much-needed respite from the Goan heat. ⊙ Candolim–Calangute Road, opposite Benetton ⊙ 0832 2282808 ⊙ midaastouch2003@yahoo.com ⓦ www.midaastouch.com ⊙ 11.00–24.00 Mon–Sun

⬤ *Eat and shop at Natural-ly*

Souza Lobo ££ **❽** A grand dame of the Calangute scene, this place is an incredible 75 years old. There's live music on Wednesday and Sunday, and it fills up quickly over the weekend. The salads and seafood are particularly recommended. ➌ On the beach, Central Calangute ❶ 0832 2281234, 0832 2276463 ❸ jude@souzalobo.com ⓦ www.souzalobo.com ⓛ 11.00–23.00 Mon–Sun

Tibetan Kitchen ££ **❾** With an excellent reputation built up over nearly 20 years, the Tibetan Kitchen is relaxed and atmospheric, serving big portions of good-value food. Magazines and board games are available, with last orders at 23.00. ➋ Set back in an alleyway off Beach Road, close to the beach ❶ 0832 2275744, 9326137750 ❸ thetibkit@yahoo.com ⓦ www.thetibetankitchen.co.uk ⓛ 09.00–14.00, 17.00–24.00 Mon–Sun, Oct–Apr

Utopia ££ **❿** Homemade ice cream and pasta produced in house by Italian chefs are two of the highlights of Utopia's impressive menu. Wooden lounge chairs and a huge golden Buddha can almost convince you you're in Thailand. ➌ Holiday Street, by the beach ❶ 0832 2282904, 9860822680 ❸ sparklinggoa@yahoo.com ⓛ 21.00–late Mon–Sun ❶ Admission charge

Waves ££ **⓫** Set in the Kerkar Art Complex, this place gives the usual Goan and Indian staples an artistic twist. As you'd expect in an art gallery, the place is designed with care and style that will delight anyone with beach-shack fatigue. ➋ Gaurawado, South Calangute ❶ 0832 2276017 ❶ 0832 2276509 ❸ subodhkerkar@satyam.net.in ⓦ www.subodhkerkar.com

RESORTS

Candolim

Just south of Baga and Calangute, Candolim is well placed enough to
have developed a decent tourist infrastructure, but removed enough to
have retained some peace, quiet and privacy. This makes it the choice for
anyone who's more likely to be up at seven in the morning because the
beach is empty at that time, rather than because they're staggering
home from a nightclub. While there are watersports to enjoy if you
wish, the main hubs for high-octane thrills in the surf are Baga and
Calangute to the north and Sinquerim to the south, which leaves
Candolim relatively free from the roar of jet-ski motors and
shrieks of air-bound tourists.

   If you've had your fill of English breakfasts and fancy some genuine
Goan fare, there are some authentic eateries among the tourist
traps. The decent selection of restaurants appeals to slightly older
holidaymakers who are no longer watching every penny, and prices are
a little higher here than in some comparable resorts. The resort is also
home to some posh designer boutiques that are a world away from the
cheap and cheerful hippie stalls in Arambol or Anjuna.

BEACHES

Compared to the next two resorts north of it, the beach at Candolim will
seem refreshingly crowd-free. Long, straight and pristine, lined by sand
dunes and palm trees, it has the postcard perfection common to Goa's
prettier resorts. It also has fewer beach shacks, which means that
between the restaurants and their plentiful sunbeds you can find empty
tracts of sand, perfect to lie down on if you're seeking a bit of solitude.
You will need your towel though – the sand can get scorching as the day
progresses. If you arrive and find you've forgotten a beach essential,
there's a small market on the approach road. You will sometimes find a
lifeguard on duty, but it cannot be guaranteed and, while swimming is
mostly safe, the sea can get rough at times.

THINGS TO SEE & DO

Meditation and yoga
Tao Zen
Iyengar-style yoga classes at 08.30 from Monday to Friday and
meditation at 17.00 Monday to Friday. Classes take place on a sea-facing
roof terrace.
🅐 Monte Villa, Murrod Vaddo, five minutes from beach
🅔 taozengoa@yahoo.co.in 🅦 www.ramayoga.com

Trips
John's Boat Tours
Up and running for 12 years, John's offers dolphin and crocodile trips,
fishing, snorkelling at Grand Island, plus trips to the Anjuna flea market

🔺 *Picture-postcard perfect*

and spice plantation, which often include a barbecue or free drinks.
ⓐ Dando ☎ 0832 6520190, 0832 2497450, 9822182814

TAKING A BREAK

Bars & cafés
Calamari £ Twinings tea is a highlight at this pleasant beach shack, where you can also rent a towel if you need one. ⓐ Dando Beach, close to Santana Beach Resort ☎ 0832 3290506, 9326102242 🕐 08.00–23.00 Mon–Sun

Chocolatti £ Indulge your sweet tooth at this family-run temple to chocolate, where cakes are baked on site. Sandwiches and salads are also available. ⓐ 409 Fort Aguada Road, opposite State Bank of India ☎ 0832 2479340, 9822001970 ⓔ rrebelo@sancharnet.in 🕐 10.00–19.00 Mon–Sat, closed Sun

AFTER DARK

Restaurants
Claudina's Beach Shack ££ This place is distinguished by a few comfy chairs that seem to belong in a grandmother's sitting room rather than a beach shack and a bookshop. ⓐ First shack to the left of beach approach road ☎ 9822158441 🕐 09.00–last customer Mon–Sun

Cuckoo Zen Garden ££ Claiming to be the only real Chinese-Taiwanese restaurant in Goa, Cuckoo Zen's cuisine is prepared and served by staff from the region, with the menu designed specifically to benefit your vital organs. Candlelit dining on the roof is another plus point. ⓐ Nana Cecilia Guest House ☎ 0832 2489570 ⓦ www.cuckoozen.com ⓔ cuckoozen@hotmail.com 🕐 19.00–23.00 Mon–Sun

Inferno ££ The inferno theme touches both the décor and the food, with flaming sizzlers a restaurant highlight. There's also a non-smoking section for those who don't want to light up, as well as an open-air part. Both the seafood and service are good. ❸ Murrodvaddo, Candolim Beach Road ☎ 0832 2276250, 9822140130 🕐 09.00–last customer Mon–Sun

Spotty's ££ Loud, lively and friendly, Spotty's has a swing seat, a pool table and a long cocktail menu. Thursday is barbecue night from 19.00, and you can also hire bikes and book boat trips here. ❸ On the beach ☎ 9822144833 🕐 08.00–24.00 Mon–Sun

Teama ££ This rooftop restaurant serves up Goan, Indian, Chinese, continental and seafood, with live music on Tuesday, Friday and Sunday from 19.30 onwards, while the air-conditioned pub below fills the gaps with karaoke on Monday and Thursday. ❸ Murrodvaddo, near Candolim Beach car park ☎ 0832 2489774 ✉ teama_since1987@yahoo.co.in 🌐 www.teamagoa.com 🕐 08.30–24.00 Mon–Sun

After Seven £££ Following a long battle with Nestlé, the owner of what was formerly known as After Eight, a graduate of Taj Hotels, admitted defeat, changed the name and opened an hour earlier. An acclaimed Goan eatery, you can watch your top-class European food being cooked in the glass-fronted kitchen. ❸ 1/274B Chapel Lane, Gaura Vaddo, off Calangute–Candolim main road ☎ 0832 2279757, 9226188288 ✉ aftersevenrestaurant@yahoo.com 🕐 18.30–23.30 Mon–Sun, 15 Oct–20 Apr ❶ Credit cards accepted

Clubs
Riio Da Hiphop Club ££ Well-regarded nightclub playing hiphop and Hindi music. ❸ Near Kingfisher Villa, Taj Aguda Road ☎ 9326169000, 9960129000

Sinquerim

Smaller than Candolim, Sinquerim is a peaceful 'end of the line' resort, with the approach road to Fort Aguada marking the close of the northern stretch of beaches. The area and its surroundings are home to two five-star resorts that set an upmarket tone and make Sinquerim one of Goa's more exclusive choices. The glut of wealthy tourists has also led to a burgeoning watersports industry, with operators competing for the business of adrenalin seekers with time and money to spend. Even if you lack the financial resources actually to stay in a five-star hotel, their restaurants, though costly by Goan standards, are within reach of most Western wallets, so Sinquerim is probably best suited to foodies with a bit of spare cash, couples without children and older tourists.

BEACHES

Populated by far fewer holidaymakers than Calangute and Baga, sloping Sinquerim Beach is quiet and relaxing. There's just one row of sunbeds and they are nicely spaced out. At high tide the stretch of sand does get narrow, but it's not busy enough for this to be a problem. Local entrepreneurs have made an effort to retain the coastline's natural charm: the majority of the beach-shack roofs and many of the umbrellas are fashioned entirely from trees. A row of palms also separates the sand from the town behind, giving a nice sense of seclusion.

THINGS TO SEE & DO

While there is obvious modernisation in the **jet-skis** that line the beach waiting for takers, the vessels you see are just as likely to be pretty, old-fashioned fishing boats bobbing along with their catch. One boat that stands out is the *River Princess*, a cargo ship that ran aground in 2000 during a monsoon and now sits just off the coast. Though from time to time there is talk of getting it moved, in true, relaxed Goan style nothing has been finalised yet, and the boat is now something of a fixture – plus a useful orientation point if you're struggling to find your sunbed again after a dip. And Sinquerim is one of the better resorts for weak swimmers, as the sea is fairly calm most of the time. If you prefer more active water-based pursuits, you'll find something to suit, whether it's jet-skiing or dolphin spotting. There's no need to search hard for a watersports *wallah* – they will find you. **Dolphin boats** also wait at the bottom of the hill leading off to Fort Aguada. Right before the hill is the Taj Holiday Village's private beach, a small section of sand separated from the main stretch by an old fortification and vantage point. Guests of the hotel enjoy not only enviable seclusion, but also rubber safety rings and the attentions of a security guard-cum-waiter.

● *Select seclusion at Sinquerim*

Massage

Ayur Kerala Ayurvedic massage therapy centre offering various treatments from 350 rupees.

⬤ *The view from Fort Aguada*

ⓐ Paradise View, opposite Taj Holiday Village ⓣ 9922233173
ⓔ ayurhome@rediff.com.
Massages are also available at the **Marquis Beach Resort** from
08.00 to 19.00. ⓐ Dando, just off the beach ⓣ 0832 2479120

AFTER DARK

Restaurants

Angela's Dolphin Inn ££ Pleasant and friendly place that does barbecues
and sells books. They can also arrange watersports for you. ⓐ Dando
Beach ⓣ 0832 5620359, 9823056352 ⓛ 08.00–23.00 Mon–Sun

Big Blue ££ Amiable staff can also organise watersports and boat trips.
ⓐ On beach below Taj Village and Fort Aguada ⓣ 9822162517,
9822001970 ⓔ bigbluegoa@yahoo.co.in ⓛ 08.00–22.00 or 23.00
Mon–Sun

The Stone House ££ The food here gets good write-ups, and the weekly
live music, sometimes jazz and blues, creates a cool atmosphere.
ⓐ Fort Aguada Road ⓣ 0832 2470090 ⓛ 07.00–24.00 Mon–Sun, Oct–Mar

Banyan Tree £££ Delightfully atmospheric Thai restaurant with tables
divided between the garden and a large gazebo overlooking the
fishpond. The food, of course, is first rate. ⓐ Taj Holiday Village ⓣ 0832
5645858 ⓛ 12.30–14.45, 19.30–22.30 Mon–Sun; lunch Sept–May only
ⓘ Credit cards accepted

Bars & clubs

Marquis £££ One of the best-looking venues in Goa, this large round
lounge club has a water feature in the middle and classy beds as well as
seats for reclining. The food is high-concept Thai, Japanese and Asian,
including sushi. It gets busy on weekends, when two or three DJs a night
play sets. ⓐ Marquis Beach Resort, Dando ⓣ 0832 2479120 ⓕ 0832
2479889 ⓔ marquis@sancharnet.in ⓛ 11.00–02.00 Mon–Sun

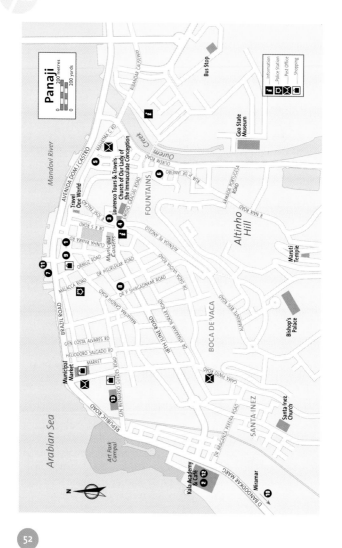

Panaji

Previously called Panjim, and sometimes still referred to as such, Goa's tiny administrative capital is around 7 km (4½ miles) from the coast, on the banks of the Mandovi River. A bustling town, it has preserved much of its Portuguese heritage, giving it a Mediterranean atmosphere. Thanks to its handiness for the airport, many people who are travelling around the state pass through Panaji at one time or another, and it's different enough from the coastal resorts to keep most of them there for a few days.

Its narrow, often pavement-less cobbled streets are sometimes calm, sometimes noisy with the sounds of trading, traffic and hooting. Colourful little houses with red-tiled roofs and some distinctive public buildings make the capital a pleasant place to stroll around. It also enjoys some of the best cultural, entertainment and dining options, which make a sophisticated change from the identikit shacks at most of the coastal resorts. Much of the action is on the Mandovi River, on whose south bank the city lies. Party boats glide up and down, pumping out bass for all they're worth; for a more serene option you can take a sunset cruise. If your holiday funds are burning a hole in your pocket, you can relieve yourself of some of them at India's only legal casino.

BEACHES

Miramar is Panaji's closest beach, just 3 km (1¼ miles) away, a 40-minute walk along Dayanand Bandodkar Marg. Swimming can be safe, but be aware that there can be undercurrents. The beach, sometimes known as Gaspar Dias, affords a good view of Fort Aguada, and you can also spot the occasional dolphin. This is an urban beach so you won't find the same pristine sand and peace as elsewhere.

Dona Paula Beach is 1 km (half a mile) further than Miramar, and often quieter. A popular film location, it offers some watersports and decent shopping. Check with the lifeguards about the undertow before swimming. Caranzalem, in between Dona Paula and Miramar, is better suited to taking the plunge as it has no undercurrents, as is Bambolim,

7 km (4¼ miles) from Panaji in the direction of Vasco, a small beach that's popular with Goans. All of these beaches are within a short tuk-tuk ride of Panaji.

THINGS TO SEE & DO

Art Park Campal
Beautifully sculpted city garden with a lake, lanterns in the trees, statues and fountains. Lit up, it's particularly pleasant for an evening stroll. From time to time it is used for art exhibitions.
ⓐ Dayanand Bandodkar Marg

Church of Our Lady of the Immaculate Conception
Bright, white and unmistakable, the church stands proudly overlooking its city, and is particularly impressive when lit up at night. Inside it is simply done out, with a Last Supper scene, two altars and statues of St Peter and St Paul. Mass in English is held at 08.00 from Monday to Friday, and at 08.30 on Sunday. The church is closed to the public during certain services.
ⓐ Emidio Gracia Road ⓣ No phone ⓛ 09.00–12.30, 15.30–17.30 Mon–Sat; 11.00–12.30, 15.30–17.00 Sun

Goa State Museum
The 12 galleries include sculpture, Christian and religious art, cultural anthropology, furniture, modern art and a photo display on Goa's fight for freedom. You can ask for a guided tour.
ⓐ EDC Complex, by Ourem Creek ⓣ 0832 2438006, 0832 2437306
ⓔ museum_goa@sancharnet.in ⓦ www.goamuseum.nic.in
ⓛ 09.30–17.30 Mon–Fri, closed Sat & Sun

Maruti Temple
If you can face the 100-plus steps required to get up there, the Maruti Temple, dedicated to the monkey god Hanuman, will reward you, both with its excellent views over Panaji and also with a cool, marble-floored place to sit and recover. If your visit coincides with the priest's

appearance, you can watch some Hindu rituals, while from 16.00 worshippers come to bathe in the water tank.

⊙ Fontainhas ⊙ 0832 2426090

Trips

Panaji is a good centre from where to book trips to other parts of the state. **Lourenco Tours & Travels** is a government-approved agency

⬟ The illuminated Church of Our Lady of the Immaculate Conception

offering trips to various resorts (from 130 rupees) and tours such as Goa by night, as well as bus services.
ⓐ Ground floor, Gama Building, near Church Square
ⓣ 0832 6511638, 9881317865

Travel One World
ⓐ Mhamai Kamat Building, near Old Secretariate ⓣ 0832 2427047, 9225901760 ⓔ sonya@traveloneworld.co.in ⓦ www.traveloneworld.net
ⓛ 09.15–19.30 or 20.00 Mon–Sat, 09.15–16.30 Sun (most but not all)

⬤ *Get great views from the Maruti Temple*

TAKING A BREAK

Cafés
Café Coffee Day £ ❶ Part of the Western-style chain serving coffees, juices, cakes, sandwiches and ice cream, this branch has a balcony. There are also outlets in Calangute and Colva. ⓐ Arthur Viegas Building, next to Hotel Law ⓔ dolly@cafecoffeeday.com ⓛ 09.00–23.00 Mon–Sun

Kala Academy Café £ ❷ Large covered café at the academy, serving a range of drinks and snacks. ⓐ Dayanand Bandodkar Marg ⓘ No phone ⓛ 09.00–20.00 or later if there is an event

Mr Baker £ ❸ Cool and airy two-level bakery with a few tables, where you can enjoy a tea, instant coffee, cake and pastry. ⓐ Opposite church, near Municipal Gardens ⓘ 0832 2224622 ⓛ 08.30–13.00, 15.30–20.00

AFTER DARK

Restaurants
George £ ❹ Small and cheerful family restaurant, which takes pains to point out that it serves both beef and pork, which other places outside the beach resorts don't for religious reasons. ⓐ Near Church of Our Lady of the Immaculate Conception ⓘ 0832 2426820, 9822487722 ⓛ 08.00–22.30 Mon–Sat, closed Sun ⓘ Credit cards accepted

Vihar £ ❺ Popular vegetarian place serving South Indian and Chinese food. Its juice bar is a big hit, as are its coconut curries. ⓐ 32 Janeiro Road by Dayanand Bandodkar Marg ⓘ 0832 2225744 ⓛ 07.00–22.00 Mon–Sun

Viva Panjim £ ❻ Getting seated and served can take time in this intimate courtyard restaurant, prettily lit and decorated with plants. There's an air-conditioned section and small terrace. The fish is particularly recommended. ⓐ 178 Rua 31 de Janeiro, Fontainhas ⓘ 0832 2422405, 9850471363 ⓛ 12.00–15.00, 19.00–22.30 Mon–Sun

Mandovi Riviera Quarterdeck ££ **7** Acclaimed riverside restaurant with a huge terrace decorated with fairy lights and a model boat. Indian, Chinese and vegetarian dishes dominate, but there's no pork or beef. Ⓐ Opposite Hotel Mandovi Ⓣ 0832 2432905, 9822154390 Ⓕ 0832 2225451 Ⓦ www.hotelmandovigoa.com/quarterdeck.htm Ⓛ 10.30–15.00 lunch, 15.30–18.30 sandwiches and salads, 19.00–23.00 dinner Mon–Sun Ⓘ Credit cards accepted

Sher-e-Punjab ££ **8** Bright and clean upmarket family eatery doing tandoori and Punjabi cuisine. Ⓐ 18th June Road Ⓣ 0832 2425657 Ⓔ butterchicken@sher-e-punjab.com Ⓛ 11.30–15.00, 18.30–22.00 Mon–Sun

Delhi Darbar £££ **9** Busy North Indian restaurant with an extensive list of vegetarian options. The upstairs floor can get very crowded, but the air conditioning makes that forgivable. Ⓐ Dayanand Bandodkar Marg Ⓣ 0832 2222544 Ⓛ 11.00–16.00, 19.00–23.00 Mon–Sun Ⓘ Credit cards accepted

Marriott restaurants £££ **10** The hotel chain's four top-quality eateries are all in one partially uncovered area, by the swimming pool. Monday, Wednesday and Friday are theme nights. Don't expect to pay Indian prices.
Coffee shop Ⓛ 24 hours Mon–Sun
Wan Hao Chinese restaurant Ⓛ 07.00–23.00 Mon–Sun
Simply Fish Ⓛ 07.00–23.00 Mon–Sun, Nov–Apr
Cake shop Ⓛ 09.00–22.30 Mon–Sun
Ⓐ Miramar Beach, Dayanand Bandodkar Marg Ⓣ 0832 2463333 Ⓕ 0832 2463300 Ⓦ marriott.com/goimc

Entertainment
Casino Goa **11** India's only live gaming casino can be worth a visit even if you have no intention of gambling. The prices are high, but your entrance fee includes drinks, and dinner if you board later. The sunset cruise is from 17.30 to 19.30 daily and costs 500 rupees; dinner is from 19.30 and will set you back 1,300 rupees from Monday to Thursday and 1,500 rupees from Friday to Sunday. There are age restrictions, so bring ID

if you look young. There's also a 'smart-casual' dress code: shorts, three-quarter-length trousers, vests (for men), flip-flops and sandals are not allowed. 🅐 Fisheries Jetty, Dayanand Bandodkar Marg 🅣 0832 2234044 🅕 0832 2234049 🅔 goacas@sancharnet.in 🅛 17.30–05.00 Mon–Thur, 17.30–06.00 Fri–Sun ❶ Admission charge

Kala Academy ⓬   Modern art academy that hosts concerts, conferences, plays, films, lectures, music and dance courses. There's also an art gallery, library, exhibition centre and a handicraft market. 🅐 Dayanand Bandodkar Marg 🅣 0832 2223280, 0832 2420452 🅦 www.kalaacademy.org

Inox Cinema ⓭   New, luxury cinema that shows both Indian films and the latest Hollywood hits. 🅐 Behind Goa Medical College, Dayanand Bandodkar Marg 🅣 0832 2420999 🅔 goa@inox.co.in 🅛 First show 11.00, last show 23.00

🔺 *Seafood heaven at the Marriott*

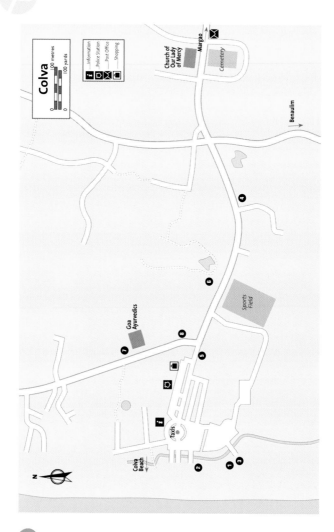

Colva

Information
Police Station
Post Office
Shopping

0 100 metres
0 100 yards

N

Colva Beach

Taxis

Goa Ayurvedics

Sports Field

Church of Our Lady of Mercy

Cemetery

Margao

Benaulim

Colva

Once a small fishing village, today Colva's entrepreneurs are more likely to be trying to hook package tourists. It's the South Goan equivalent of Calangute, although not as developed. There's enough tourist-oriented nightlife for the place to feel like a proper resort, but it's less of a clubber's magnet than some of the northern resorts, and is consequently popular with a slightly older crowd of holidaymakers, who like their nights out but also want to be in bed before the sun comes up. Plenty of independent market stalls compete with the more high-end shops for your custom, and many of them stay open late into the evening, which means the resort is lively for most of the time, and does not have that post-beach, pre-dinner lull that some smaller places do. It's not the smartest town on the coast, but has an unpolished charm that can appeal to the laidback traveller. Much of the activity is centred on a big concrete circle; in one direction this leads to the road to Margao and in the other to two small concrete bridges over which lies the beach.

BEACHES

Although now overshadowed by tourism, fishing still plays an important role in Colvan life. There's often some sort of fish-related activity going on at the beach, and early risers can sometimes see the catch being brought in. Most of the activity takes place near the bridges, where the fish vans await their loads and the beach shacks are concentrated. There are also a few funfair-type stalls here. If you're after more seclusion, walk for a few hundred metres; the beach shacks and sunbathers soon thin out. The clean, palm-fringed beach is not particularly wide, but seldom feels too crowded, although more Indian tourists tend to arrive over the weekend and at peak holiday time.

As well as a volleyball net for those who fancy a little beach exercise, some watersports are available in Colva, with the dolphin trip operators particularly dynamic in trying to put tourist bums on their boat seats. However, if you're lucky, you might not even need to take to sea – the dolphins occasionally venture near enough to the shore to be visible from your sunbed. The long, uninterrupted stretch of sand around Colva is also good for walkers. Go left along the beach and you'll come to the quieter Benaulim, right and you will ultimately reach the entirely untouristy Majorda. At night the shoreline becomes lively, with many of the beach shacks trying to outdo each other with their live music.

THINGS TO SEE & DO

Ayurveda
Goa Ayurvedics
ⓐ Next to Sea Pearl Restaurant, Longuinos Road, Colva
ⓦ www.goaayurvedics.com

Church of Our Lady of Mercy
Contains a statue of Baby Jesus, whose finger – attached from a previous statue removed by the Christians – is said to grant miracles. Chief among the hopeful are young singletons seeking a partner. ⓐ Colva Beach Road, opposite the post office

TAKING A BREAK

Sun Sea & Sand £ ❶   With a good range of juices, milk shakes, lassis, cocktails and 'mocktails', this no-frills beach shack is well placed for you to take on liquids between swimming and sunbathing. ⓐ Colva Beach
ⓣ 0832 2789077 ⓔ antonioseasun@goatelecom.com

AFTER DARK

Oceanic Seafront Haven £ ❷   Popular with local families as well as tourists, Oceanic is a great place to sit and watch the fishermen go about their work. The service is good, and they are currently arranging internet access. ⓐ On the beach, to left of approach road ⓣ 9923331320
ⓔ mohdrafeekak@yahoo.com ⓛ 08.00–24.00 or last customer Mon–Sun

◒ The palm-fringed resort of Colva

Luke's Place £ ❸ With a hookah pipe (and 24 flavours to smoke from it), plus comfy sofas and a bright mural on the back wall, Luke's has a relaxed, slightly alternative vibe. ❸ Beachfront, fifth shack on right from approach road ❶ 9890225436 ❸ 09.30–23.00 Mon–Sun

▲ Head out for a spot of dolphin-watching

Gatsby's ££ ❹ The only stand-alone pub and disco in South Goa, Gatsby's also has a 24-hour coffee shop. Peak time is between 21.00 and 03.00. ➋ Colva Beach Road, next to UTI Bank ➊ 0832 2789745 ⏰ 24 hours Mon–Sun

Goodman's ££ ❺ Run by a Norwegian woman and her Indian husband, Goodman's draws in holidaymakers with its live music – check notice board for bands and karaoke – and sports events on the big screen. It's simply decorated with a few pictures on the wall, and there's a pool table and dartboard. ➋ Colva Beach Road ➊ 0832 2788041 ⏰ 08.00–last customer Mon–Sun

Mickey's ££ ❻ Popular and unpretentious place catering to a fun-loving, foreign crowd. Unlike a lot of places, Mickey's offers lamb dishes. ➋ UBI's Pride Apartments, near football ground ➊ 0832 2789125 ✉ mickeyscolvagoa@yahoo.co.in ⏰ 11.30–15.00, 18.30–01.00 Mon–Sun

Sea Pearl ££ ❼ Highly reputed meat-oriented eatery whose pretty fairy lights and lively atmosphere make it a good choice for dinner. As well as the seafood, some of the continental staples are not half bad. ➋ Opposite Vista-de-Colva ➊ 0832 2730070 ⏰ 08.30–14.00, 18.00–23.00 Mon–Sun

Tate Sports Bar ££ ❽ Brand-new family restaurant trying to bring a touch of sophistication to seaside dining with leather seats and a sand-free tiled floor. The menu, currently being developed, will cater mainly for the English palate and adds nice touches like unlimited tea refills. There's a play area with beanbags for children and a TV showing sport for the adults. ➋ 1 Amrut Building, 4th Ward ➊ 9823615104 ✉ emmaandtoff@hotmail.com ⏰ 09.00–23.00 Mon–Sun

Benaulim

Understated Benaulim offers beauty at bargain prices. Despite its
proximity to Colva, it is far more serene and relaxed, and many visitors
to this resort stay on for weeks or even longer. The nightlife is on the
low-key side, and while the place is certainly on the road to greater
development, for now you can still enjoy the 'real Goa' here. Larger hotels
are only just beginning to appear alongside the paddy fields and
ramshackle cottages that give the town its rural feel. That's not to say
that everything about Benaulim is low budget and basic. The Taj Exotica
ensures that there is plenty of classy dining if you want it. At the other
end of the scale, a small Kashmiri market is growing up around the
crossroads area in the middle of the village.

BEACHES

Flecked with fishing boats and the odd cow ambling along, Benaulim's
beach is a haven of calm. The small approach road hosts a modest
market with beach essentials such as flip-flops, sun hats, t-shirts and
Frisbees. You can also pick up your postcards, some Ayurvedic medicine
and a coconut juice there. Once you get to the beach, you'll have little
trouble finding an empty sunbed. If you want even more seclusion,
wander left past the half dozen or so beach shacks, and you may pretty
much have the sand to yourself, apart from the odd approach from
the occasional beach trader. To the right, about 3 km (1¼ miles) away,
is the more hectic resort of Colva. Weekends and holiday times can be
slightly busier, as the beach is a favourite with Indian holidaymakers.
The sea is safe for swimming, but it's recommended you stick to the
designated area, where the lifeguard sometimes patrols. A flag
system is in operation.

THINGS TO SEE & DO

Manthan

This converted 15-room turn-of-the-century manor is now run as a heritage gallery, where you can pick up furniture, art, antiques and clothes. Shopping here is not cheap, but the place is worth a look round, even if your budget doesn't stretch to actually buying anything.

 1346 Manzil Vaddo, near Holy Trinity Church 0832 2771659

Watersports

Colva is the local centre for watersports, but you can still do some activities from Benaulim.

 Blissful Benaulim

Dolphin trips leave **Pele's Water Sports** at 08.00 and 09.00. Fishing, banana-boat trips, jet-skiing and parasailing can also be arranged.
☎ 9822080045

TAKING A BREAK

Taj Exotica Poolside sandwich counter and juice bar The place for an upmarket poolside lunch. There's a daily health drink for the diet conscious and ice cream for the less so. ✆ Hotel Taj Exotica
☎ 0832 2771234 ◷ 09.00–19.00 Mon–Sun ❶ Credit cards accepted

◮ *A beach vendor at Benaulim*

AFTER DARK

Pedro's £ A Benaulim veteran, brightly coloured Pedro's started up in 1969. A British musician plays live on Tuesday while on Saturday it's the turn of a Goan performer to take to the stage. There's a small dance floor, an extensive menu, and the place also organises dolphin trips departing at 08.00 and 09.30. ⓐ By entrance from road ⓣ 9822389177 ⓛ 08.30–01.30 Mon–Sun

Coco's ££ Professionally run shack that hosts live music and dancing on Monday night with a UK singer, plus a barbecue, fireworks and bonfire from 20.30. Look out for the fish dishes and for the cocktail specials. ⓐ Second beach shack on right from car park ⓣ 9890348045, 9890229007 ⓛ 08.00–01.00 Mon–Sun

Roger's Hygienic Kitchen ££ With a slightly Moroccan feel to it, Roger's has a charity bookshop, pool table and comfy chairs. Friday nights have live music, and the menu contains a useful explanation of Indian terms. ⓐ Third beach shack on right from car park ⓣ 9822488079 ⓔ rogfer91@hotmail.com, rogerfernandes2000@yahoo.com ⓛ 06.00–last customer (around 01.00–03.00) Mon–Sun

Lobster Shack £££ One of the always impressive Taj Hotel restaurants, this beachfront eatery offers exquisitely prepared fresh fish alongside a live seafood display and open kitchen. Expect the prices to be as international as the standards. ⓐ Hotel Taj Exotica ⓣ 0832 2771234 ⓛ 11.00–18.00 snack bar menu, 19.30–22.45 Mon–Sun ⓘ Credit cards accepted

Palolem

So flawless is Palolem that the last time you saw anything similar you were probably looking at a double-spread in a holiday brochure. The village enjoys the reputation of having the most beautiful beach in Goa, and as you lie on the gently curving stretch of pristine sand bordered by hills and palms, watching picturesque fishing boats bobbing on the calm sea, it's hard to disagree. One of the state's southernmost resorts, it's been spared the worst excesses of tourist development, and retains a laidback charm that's apparent in the hippie clothes, spice and book stalls on the road leading to the beach. You won't often see books on sale in Goa's resorts, and their presence is indicative of the kind of traveller who pitches up here: one who intends to stick around a while and enjoy the quiet and serenity – plus some of the most exquisite sunsets the state can offer.

BEACHES

The sea here is generally the preserve of fishermen and of swimmers enjoying the gradual slope of the seabed and calm waters. Be aware that there are some undertows, especially at the southern end of the beach; there are signs directing you to a specified bathing area and you will often find a lifeguard on duty. Other water-based activities are pretty much limited to boogie boarding and surfing, or dolphin spotting with one of the local fishermen – and there's a volleyball net on the sand.

But few visitors are here to exert themselves. If you're lying on the beach or taking on refreshments at one of the small beach shacks, you don't even have to get up to buy a book: the book *wallah* will come to you. Ditto the taxi drivers and boat operators, who congregate at the entrance to the beach.

Although protected from over-exploitation by its distance from the other main resorts, Palolem has increasingly become part of the tourist trail in recent years. For more solitude, head south: the secluded **Patnam**, **Colomb** and **Rajbag** beaches are all within walking distance.

THINGS TO SEE & DO

Ayurveda
Bhakti Kutir Ayurveda Centre

Choose from massages, detox, consultations with an Ayurvedic doctor, yoga classes, meditation and a circus theatre workshop. There are also lessons for children and language lessons for adults in Hindi and Konkani.

296 Colomb, 200 m (660 ft) from beach ☎ 0832 2643469
bhaktikutir@yahoo.com www.bhaktikutir.com

Blue Planet

As well as running yoga classes every day at 09.00, and at 16.00 on Monday, Wednesday and Friday, the Blue Planet supplements its

Charm and beauty: Palolem

wellbeing services by serving a range of health foods, including fruit, local vegetables, homemade bread and tofu.
ⓐ Main Street ⓣ 9850456228, 9860656541 ⓔ monika@alloneness.com
ⓛ 09.00–17.00 15 Oct–15 April

Palolem Ayurvedic Centre
English-run centre that's praised for both its services and its prices.
ⓐ Behind Hotel Good Shepherd ⓣ 9422640193
ⓔ palolemayurvediccentre@yahoo.co.in

TAKING A BREAK

Brown Bread £ Very popular vegetarian-health food emporium dishing up tofu, wheatgrass, muesli and the like. ⓐ Main Road ⓣ 0832 2643604

AFTER DARK

Bars, cafés & restaurants
Café del Mar ££ One of the few places in Goa that offers Thai cuisine, Café del Mar serves food until 23.00 and shows live football on its TV.
ⓐ On the beach ⓣ 0832 2276493 ⓛ 24 hours Mon–Sun

Casa Fiesta ££ An unusual Mexican place, this popular eatery has a pleasantly lit garden, Latin music and a mellow atmosphere.
ⓐ Main Road ⓣ 0832 6470368 ⓛ 08.00–23.00 or last customer Mon–Sun

Cheeky Chapatti ££ An English-run eatery – as the comedy name suggests – this place has a laidback atmosphere, and serves sandwiches and wraps as well as seafood, vegetarian and pasta dishes. ⓐ Main Road
ⓣ 9326137628 ⓛ 09.30–22.30 for food; bar open later Mon–Sun

Ciarans ££ Classy beachside hotel restaurant with plush black leather chairs and wooden decking. There's a big book collection and board games to entertain you. Great value and top quality. ⓐ On beach

☎ 0832 2643477, 0832 2644074 ✉ hello@ciarans.com,
johnciaran@hotmail.com 🌐 www.ciarans.com 🕐 06.30–23.00 Mon–Sun,
last order 22.30

Cuba ££ A mainstay of the Palolem scene, trendy Cuba plays loud,
mellow music as its customers relax on bean bags with games and
books or watching sport on the TV. Its various theme nights include a
barbecue on Friday, lobster on Saturday and jumbo prawns on Sunday
(book ahead). There is also occasional live music and DJs, as well as
singles and gay nights and pool competitions. In addition to playing your
CDs and teaching you cookery, they'll book you on a bus, train, plane,
boat or day trip and can even plan your wedding. The food is excellent
too. There is another outlet open year-round on Palolem High Street.
📍 On beach ☎ 9822183775 🕐 08.00–02.00 Mon–Sun
✉ dearholidays@rediffmail.com

🔻 *Dinner on the beach: a perfect end to the day*

Cyrus beach café ££ Romantic option for a nightcap with two-seater tables on the beach. Serves the usual selection of food, with the addition of Thai. ❸ On the beach ❶ 0832 2644065, 9823102168 ❸ 07.00–01.00 or 02.00 Mon–Sun

Dropadi ££ Plusher-than-average beach shack with fans, some glass tables and bright, cheerful décor. It has a well-stocked bar and cocktail menu. Last orders at 22.45. ❸ Corner of road and beach ❶ 9423821181 ❸ sanjaybick@rediffmail.com ⓦ www.goyam.net ❸ 07.30–23.00 Mon–Sun

Magic Italy ££ Run by an Italian chef who imports ingredients from home, the pizzas and pastas are made in house. Magic Italy is bright and colourful, with plants and a pleasant area at the back with cushions. They stick to their area of expertise: Italian food. ❸ Main Street, 50 m (160 ft) from entrance to beach ❶ 9822381457 ❸ 18.00–23.00 Mon–Sun

Sabai Sabai ££ Friendly and authentic trattoria. Both chef and pizza *wallah* are Italian and you can watch your pizza emerge from the oven. The pasta too is homemade. Dinner, which also includes a few Indian choices, is served from 18.00. ❸ Main Road, next to Hotel Good Shepherd ❶ 9860900173 ❸ 09.00–23.00 Mon–Sun

World Kitchen Siona ££ The World Kitchen has a warm and friendly atmosphere, small tables around which you sit on the floor and occasional live music. It is big on seafood, and its Italian fare comes recommended. ❸ Main Street, 50m (160 ft) from entrance to beach ❶ 9822176966, 9822155815 ❸ 08.30–late Mon–Sun

❶ *A bird's-eye view of Fort Aguada*

EXCURSIONS
Out & about

Bardez taluka

Made up of 12 villages plus its capital city, **Mapusa**, Bardez taluka provides a glimpse of a Goa that has nothing to do with tourism, development or cash. A largely rural district, there is no one main attraction: the enjoyment is in driving around – it would be difficult to explore without your own transport – and popping into the tiny temples, churches and villages that you happen upon. In this part of the state, tourists are still a novelty, and you may find yourself something of a curiosity.

GETTING THERE

To get started, take an east turning from National Highway 17, which runs between Panaji and Mapusa. Any local tuk-tuk or taxi driver should know some of the prettier and more interesting spots.

THINGS TO SEE & DO

Houses of Goa Museum
Housed in an interesting modern building that looks more like a boat, this place showcases Goan architecture through maps, designs and plans, some of which are over 500 years old. There's a slide show at 19.00 and a pleasant café on the ground floor.

❸ Torda, Salvador-do-Mundo village ❶ 0832 2410711 ❺ 0832 2410709

✉ archauto@sancharnet.in ⓦ www.archgoa.org 🕐 10.00–19.30

Tues–Sun, closed Mon ❶ Admission charge

TAKING A BREAK

There are few formal eating options outside Mapusa.

Golden Oven £ Clean and well-run bakery. Cakes and pastries are made and presented with great care. The breakfasts are also highly recommended. ❸ Mapusa, by the market 🕐 09.00–18.30

Heera Snacks and Ice Cream £ Ideally situated if you're just getting on or off a bus and want some light refreshments. ❷ Mapusa, north of the roundabout, opposite the bus station ❶ No phone ⏲ 08.00–12.00, 16.00–24.00

AFTER DARK

Tequila £ Rooftop eatery with simple Indian and Goan fare. ❷ Mapusa, Hotel Vilena ❶ 0832 2263115

🔺 *Mapusa market*

Fort Aguada

Now nearly 400 years old, Aguada was a key fort during the Portuguese occupation, and enjoyed such a superb strategic location that it was never taken by force. Now a protected monument, the fort enjoys splendid views over the coast, and is especially enchanting at sunset. The well-preserved stronghold is hugely popular, particularly with Indian tourists, and part of the pleasure of a visit is in receiving shy requests for photographs and chats with the local people.

GETTING THERE

Energetic and hardy types can reach the fort on foot by a trail that starts at Marbella Guesthouse, but it's a very steep 2-km (1¼-mile) climb. Otherwise the 4-km (2½-mile) journey from Sinquerim can be done by bicycle, motorcycle or taxi.

THINGS TO SEE & DO

Most visitors make for the old bastion, on the top of the hill. Here you can see the enormous subterranean water tanks that would have sustained the fort in the event of a long siege. The old four-storey Portuguese lighthouse is another point of interest, said to be the oldest of its kind in India. The new lighthouse is open to visitors from 16.00 to 17.30 for a small charge.

TAKING A BREAK

Once you get to the main bastion itself, there is little in the way of refreshment, apart from a couple of stalls selling sweet or salty lime sodas and coconut juice, but the approach road to Fort Aguada has plenty of dining options.

The Portuguese stronghold of Fort Aguada

Sweet Chilli ££ This garden restaurant has a lively atmosphere boosted by regular theme nights. Outside the holiday season it's only open over the weekend. The food comes highly recommended. ❷ Off the Taj Fort Aguada junction ☎ 0832 2479446

The Curry House ££ With a pleasant, mellow atmosphere and occasional live music, the Curry House dishes up the typical range of food with an emphasis – obviously – on curry. ❷ Fort Aguada Road, near Kingfisher Villa, Dando ☎ 9890481096 🕑 09.00–24.00

Morisco £££ A daily-changing menu and an open kitchen are two of the draws at this superior, seafood restaurant. There's live entertainment in the evenings from October to March. After dinner, transfer to the Martini Bar for poolside cocktails. ❷ Fort Aguada Beach Resort ☎ 0832 6645858 🕑 12.30–15.00, 19.30–23.00, Martini Bar 10.30–24.00 ❶ Credit cards accepted

Dr Salim Ali Bird Sanctuary

Providing sanctuary not only for Goa's feathered friends, this wildlife reserve also offers human visitors a respite from the noise and bustle of the resorts. Taking its name from the so-called 'Birdman of India', the country's most famous ornithologist, the bird sanctuary makes a good half-day trip. Bird lovers have the more obvious reasons to go there, but floating slowly around the creeks in a boat, with no other human in sight apart from your boatman, offers an enchanting glimpse of rural India.

GETTING THERE

Getting there requires some effort. Take the ferry from Ribandar, 4 km (2½ miles) from Panaji, across the Mandovi to Chorao island. They run every ten minutes in each direction from 06.00–02.00. From the disembarking point you can walk to the sanctuary. Buy your ticket at the small office to the left.

ⓐ By ferry wharf **ⓘ** No phone **ⓦ** No website **ⓛ** Office open 09.00–17.00 **ⓘ** Admission charge

THINGS TO SEE & DO

To make the most out of your trip, it's best to hire a boatman, who will probably be hanging around at the wharf waiting for tourists. After negotiating a price, he'll take you to the vessel, a hollowed-out mango tree that can hold up to four passengers. The sanctuary itself is less than 200 hectares (494 acres) in total but, despite its small size, is home to some 400 different bird species, among which you're likely to spot egrets, cormorants, herons, kingfishers, kites, eagles and woodpeckers. The odd otter, jackal or crocodile may also be visible. A good viewing point is the bird-watching tower, but access to this is dependent on the water level.

Perhaps because it's somewhat out of the way, few tourists reach the sanctuary, and you may well find you are sharing the mangrove-lined waterways only with the wildlife you're there to see and the odd fishing boat attending to its nets.

The sanctuary is open all year round, but is at its best – in terms both of birds and of heat and humidity – from October to March or April. The ideal time of day to visit is early in the morning, from 06.00 to 09.00, and from 17.00 until dusk. Not having a constant stream of tourists, there are no real facilities to speak of, but you can find a few places to stop for a tea or a juice, usually open from around 06.30 to 20.30.

TAKING A BREAK

Tukram Mandrekar fresh lime soda shop £ Small, no-frills place where you can pick up a fresh lime soda. ② Near ferry ⏰ 8.00–20.30

⬤ *Crocodiles are among the wildlife visible at the sanctuary*

Old Goa

Old Goa is the antidote to the undemanding beach life – here you will find culture and history in spades. In its heyday, the city, chosen by the Portuguese as their capital, was the size of London, and rivalled Lisbon in its greatness. But while what stands today is not on that scale, Old Goa's buildings are impressive enough to capture the grandeur of its history; its churches and convents are listed as a UNESCO World Heritage Site. The attractions, mostly opulent churches, are centred on a large, neat green. Be warned – there is very little shade when walking between them.

GETTING THERE

The town is 9 km (5½ miles) east of Panaji, from where you can pick up a bus at the Kadamba bus stand. They depart frequently and take just under half an hour. You can also continue by bus to Ponda.

THINGS TO SEE & DO

Archaeology Museum
Sculptures, paintings and fragments, mostly with a religious theme, are on display. Some exhibits date back over 2,000 years. Children under 15 go in for free. ❸ Adjoining the Church of St Francis of Assisi
🕓 10.00–17.00 Sat–Thur, closed Fri ❶ Admission charge

Basilica of Bom Jesus
Probably the most impressive of Old Goa's churches, the basilica contains the remains of St Francis Xavier. The 17th-century baroque building has marble floors and richly gilded altars.
ⓐ 100 m (330 ft) south of Old Goa Road 🕓 06.30–19.00 Mon–Sun

Bom Jesus Basilica Art Gallery
The Bom Jesus Basilica Art Gallery is the largest gallery of modern church art in Asia, featuring paintings commissioned and executed in the 1970s.

🔵 Upstairs at Basilica of Bom Jesus Ⓦ www.dommartin.cc
🕐 09.00–17.00 Wed–Mon, closed Tues

Church of St Francis of Assisi
This high-ceilinged church has a stunning interior, thanks to both its gold and the big paintings on the walls.
🔵 250 m (820 ft) north of Old Goa Road, in between Chapel of St Catherine and Se Cathedral 🕐 09.00–17.30 Mon–Sun

⬥ *The Church of St Francis of Assisi*

Kristu Kala Mandir Art Gallery

Much of the religious art here is of a modern bent, including the life-size wax model of the Last Supper. There's a pleasant garden at the back.

🅰 Adjoining the Se Cathedral 🕒 09.30–17.30 Tues–Sun, closed Mon
ⓘ Admission charge

🔺 *The striking Se Cathedral*

Se Cathedral

The largest church in Asia has a striking white and gold interior, stone floor, and houses the cross of miracles, on which shepherds are said to have seen an apparition of Christ in 1619. ⓐ In same complex as Church of St Francis of Assisi ⓛ 06.30–17.30 Mon–Sun

TAKING A BREAK

Asi Canteen £ With a couple of tables, this is one of the only oases in the middle of Old Goa where you can recover with a snack and a drink and take refuge from the unrelenting sun. ⓐ By Se Cathedral ⓛ 06.00–19.00 Mon–Sun

Solar Souto Maior £ It would be a shame to come without seeing this place, a true highlight of Old Goa. Formerly part of a Portuguese palace, it has retained its stateliness, and is now a delightful complex. The three tables on the charming terrace are nicely spaced out to allow you some privacy. The reasonably priced food is excellent, with the almond soup quite exquisite. You can buy or drink a range of luxury teas in the tearoom, or pick up expensive pashminas, clothes, furniture or gifts from the shop. ⓐ Peres House, HNo B40, St Pedro, 1.5 km (1 mile) from Old Goa ⓣ 0832 5614524, 9326127675 ⓦ www.solargoa.in ⓛ Café from 10.00–18.00 Mon–Sun

Ponda

For the tourist, Ponda is about two things: temples and spices.
There are five important temples in Ponda, rebuilt after destruction
by the Portuguese. Its spice farms are among the few tourist
enterprises in the state that go about their business with true Western
values: tours are well organised, informative and entertaining. Ponda
itself is industrial and busy with traffic and traders, something of a
culture shock after the laidback resorts, although unexpectedly
beautiful monuments and statues punctuate the factories and
industrial parks.

THINGS TO SEE & DO

Spice farms

Sahakari Spice Farm
Very well-organised facility that offers fascinating interactive tours
of the spice farm followed by a buffet lunch, for 300 rupees. It's very
touristy, but the professional and knowledgeable guides give you a
great time. On Wednesday, Saturday and Sunday you can also have an
Ayurveda body massage, and elephant rides and feeding are sometimes
possible behind the farm.
Ⓐ Ponda belgaum Highway Curti ☎ 0832 2312394, 9850466478
🖷 0832 2319826 ✉ info@sahakarifarms.com Ⓦ www.sahakarifarms.com
🕙 09.00–16.00; last entrance around 14.00

Savoi Plantation
Ⓐ Savoi, Ponda ☎ 0832 2340272 Ⓦ www.savoiplantations.com

Tropical Spice Plantation
Ⓐ Arla Bazar, Keri ☎ 0832 2340329
✉ tropicalspiceplantation@rediffmail.com 🕙 08.00–17.00

Temples

Ponda managed to elude Portuguese control for two and a half centuries after the arrival of the Europeans, and Hindus fleeing persecution elsewhere in the state built the temples to house the deities they had

◆ *Ride or feed an elephant at Sahakari Spice Farm...*

managed to bring with them. The best one is probably Sri Manguesh Temple, off the National Highway 4A, a big complex with chandeliers and a lamp tower. Less than 2 km (1¼ miles) away is Shri Mahalsa, a Vishnu temple boasting what is said to be the biggest oil lamp in the world outside it. Shantadurga Temple, less than 5 km (3 miles) from the town centre, is one of the biggest and most highly renowned in the state. Its chandelier and polished marble floors and pillars are striking features of it.

TAKING A BREAK

Niranjan Sweet Mart £ It's more of a shop than a sit-in place, but the helpful employees will be delighted to furnish you with a selection of their traditional Indian sweets and cakes. ❸ Bhavani Sadan, Upper Bazaar ❶ 0832 2314412

⬤ ...then break for a buffet

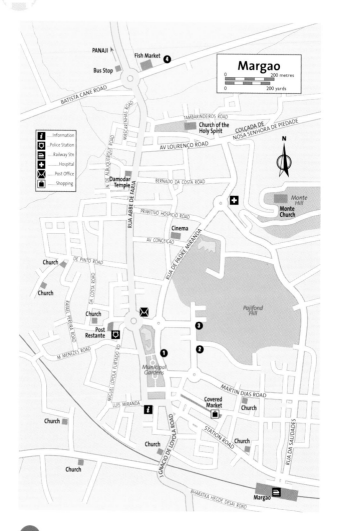

Margao
0   200 metres
0   200 yards

Information
Police Station
Railway Stn
Hospital
Post Office
Shopping

Margao

Hectic Margao makes few concessions to tourism, and as such is a good way to experience authentic Indian daily life. There's a couple of markets – with not a hippie bag in sight, some religious sites, plus plenty of Portuguese architecture. All this combines to form a microcosm of Goa as it is outside the beach resorts. If you're heading south by car or bus you're almost certain to pass through Margao, and it's well worth making a short stop.

THINGS TO SEE & DO

Covered market
The sights, smells and sounds of old India will besiege you in Margao's vibrant covered market. Spices and fruit are piled up alongside flower

◆ *Portuguese architecture is among Margao's attractions*

◆ *Statuette at Damodar Temple*

garlands and sweets plus a miscellany of practical items like saris, clothes and kitchenware. Goan matriarchs thread through the narrow walkways between stalls, which are crammed in so tightly that the vendors are often sitting atop them with their goods. As much performance artist as vendor, watch out for the coconut juice man, whose skills with a machete border on the scary – beware of bits of flying coconut.

ⓐ Rua F de Loiola, south of Municipal Gardens ● 08.00–20.00 Mon–Sat

Damodar Temple

Colourful temple whose paper flags hanging from the ceiling and portraits on the wall distinguish it from the norm. The priest is there from 07.00–09.00 and 20.30–22.00.

ⓐ Abade Faria Road ⓘ No phone ● 07.30–22.00 Mon–Sun

Fish market

It's unlikely you'll want to buy anything from the fish market, but if you're in the area, which is likely due to its proximity to the bus station, do take a look: it provides a real glimpse of authentic Goan life.

ⓐ North of roundabout, opposite bus station ● Irregular

Municipal Gardens

Margao's pretty gardens are a small haven from the bustle of city life, and sleepy Margaons can often be seen having a lie-down in the shade. There's a water feature, a variety of flowers and benches, as well as a children's play area.

ⓐ Between Abade Faria Road and Padre Miranda Road, south of the post office ● 07.30–20.30 Mon–Sun

TAKING A BREAK

Café Marliz £ ❶ This quirkily decorated café doesn't serve main meals, but it's a decent place to have a juice. ⓐ Next to Municipal Gardens ● 15.00–19.30 Mon–Sun

AFTER DARK

Banjara ££ ❷ Air-conditioned Banjara, one of the city's best restaurants, is a stylish option: the attention to detail in both the décor and food is very evident. ❷ D'Souza Chambers, Valaulikar Road, east of Municipal Gardens ☎ 0832 2714837, 0832 2722008 🕓 11.00–15.00, 19.00–23.00 Mon–Sun

Gaylin ££ ❶ This newly renovated Chinese restaurant is done out with the required lanterns, dragons and so on. It's a relaxed place to eat with a pleasant staff, and the air-conditioned ground floor is a big draw. ❷ Shar-N-Shorai Building, Valauliker Road ☎ 0832 2733348 ✉ gaylin@goacom.com 🕓 11.00–15.00, 19.00–23.00 Mon–Sun

Damodar's ££ ❹ Clean, simple and air-conditioned, this family restaurant serves Goan, Indian and Chinese meals with a lot of fish. Cool down afterwards with an ice cream or juice. ❷ First floor of complex opposite fish market ☎ 0832 2700511 🕓 11.00–16.00, 19.00–23.00 Mon–Sun

◗ *Colourful crafts reflect Goan culture*

LIFESTYLE

Food & drink

Like its architecture, festivals, religions and much else besides, Goa's food is a mélange of different influences. On the one hand, it's part of India, and the nation's love of eye-watering spices, rice, lentils and chutneys informs Goan gastronomy. On the other hand, the state often has the feel of an island, and its distinct identity is also reflected in local dishes, as is the huge natural resource to which Goan restaurateurs have unlimited access: the sea. Even inland Goa is dissected by rivers, and fish is a staple of the state's cuisine.

The classic dish is probably prawn curry, which you'll see on practically every menu in every resort. Other fish curries are also popular, and the Portuguese have also influenced the way Goans eat fish: *caldeirada* (fish stew with various vegetables and herbs cooked in wine) and *recheiado* (fried fish with a spicy masala filling) are two gastronomic colonial legacies. Sea creatures that could end up on your plate include kingfish, tuna, shark, rockfish, sardines, pomfret, mackerel, squid and mussels. Many restaurants can also do you tiger prawns or lobster, provided that you order in advance; some dedicate one night of the week to each.

Committed carnivores should not be put off by India's love of vegetarianism: there's plenty of meat available. While beef is forbidden to Hindus and pork to Muslims, the relaxed Goans seem to place more emphasis on hospitality than asceticism, and most restaurants in tourist resorts, especially the larger establishments, offer both. Chicken also appears extensively on menus, as do goat (sometimes listed as mutton) and – to a lesser extent – lamb. Cooking methods are a mixture of traditional Indian and Portuguese. Many of the dishes are heavily spiced (pepper, garlic, chillies, turmeric, coriander, cumin and ginger pop up fairly frequently), although Goan waiters are aware that foreign palates are not as robust as their own, and meals may be prepared far less piquantly than the authentic version. Of course, if your tongue is up to the challenge, they will happily cook you up a local spice-fest too. Spice devotees who are keen to learn more about Goan seasoning should head to one of the spice farms in Ponda.

⬥ *Fresh from the sea: gorgeous Goan fish*

As in the rest of India, the rule is pretty much 'rice with everything'. Rice is a staple, and is also the best treatment if you've just inadvertently bitten into a particularly tear-inducing chilli. As well as being served separately, rice is also an integral part of many dishes such as the Muslim biryani. Vegetables too play a big part, often in the form of lentils and pulses (*dhal*) or chutneys and relishes, which can also be on the hot side.

While Goa's spicier offerings can be friend or foe to the traveller, there will be few visitors to the state who won't delight in the variety and quality of fruit on offer. The fresh pineapples, watermelons, mangos, papayas and coconuts available are far superior to the versions that make it onto Western supermarket shelves. Buy fruit from one of the women who wander the beaches with baskets of it on their head, or sample it in the many juices, milkshakes, smoothies or lassis on offer in almost every eatery. The fruit alone may be enough to keep your sweet tooth satisfied, but, if not, the local desserts include *bebinca* (baked coconut pancakes that are required eating at all Goan celebrations), *dodol* (a sweet and sticky flour snack also with coconuts and cashews) and *kulkuls* (a deep fried dough featuring – as usual – coconut). If you pass a sweet shop – which is fairly likely, as there are plenty of them around – it's well worth asking for a selection box. There are familiar options such as shortbread and marzipan, and there are plenty of other delicacies that will go down well with everyone, especially with children.

When it comes to drinks, tea is king. Goans – indeed almost all Indians – love their *chai*, and you'll often see the *chai wallah* weaving his way through the street or market with a tray of tea for the traders. Tea in India is milky and indescribably sugary. If that's not to your taste, make sure you ask for the milk and sugar separately – most of the better restaurants will bring it that way automatically. The domination of tea means that coffee takes something of a back seat. It's usually available, although it is not likely to be anything more inspiring than a cup of Nescafé; however, some of the better cafés are waking up to the fact that many tourists enjoy their coffee, and now serve a decent cup of filter coffee, espresso or cappuccino.

If you're after something cold, the traditional Indian choice is the lassi, a yoghurt drink that can come in sweet or savoury forms and in

Goa is often flavoured with fruit. Because of the heat you'll probably be taking a lot of water on board as well; some eateries give you a complimentary bottle with your food. Juices are ubiquitous, and smoothies and shakes can also be found on most menus. It's worth trying a coconut juice as much for the show as for the drink itself: the vendor will thwack lumps off the fruit with a huge and rather frightening knife before piercing it with a straw. When you've finished the juice, he will then cut it open for you to eat the flesh.

With a taste more akin to paint stripper than anything else, *feni*, the local spirit, is best downed in one. If you prefer your drinks less potent, beer is widely available, with Kingfisher the most popular brand among

△ *Working the paddy fields*

tourists. Not subject to the same taxes as it is in the rest of India, it's relatively cheap. Perhaps because of the temperatures, there's less demand for wine, but you can find it in some of the more upmarket restaurants. Much of the liquor consumed in Goa is in the form of cocktails, and most beach shacks will have an extensive list, both alcoholic and non-alcoholic.

You can start eating early in Goa; most places open for breakfast at 07.00 or 08.00, some even earlier. The vast majority of restaurants and cafés serve main meals and snacks until 23.00, or later. There's little to choose between the majority of places, which all do English (and sometimes Israeli) breakfasts, sandwiches and salads, plus standard Indian, Goan, Chinese and continental mains, the latter usually consisting of some pizza and pasta dishes then variations on meat and two veg. Prices are fairly uniform and few places attempt to offer something above and beyond the norm – which means those that do are truly special (and expensive).

Pretty much everything is done with the tourist in mind. While Indians eschew cutlery to eat with their right hands, this is not expected of foreign customers, and you would have to go to the smallest, most off-the-beaten-track local establishment to find a menu that wasn't in English. Non-smokers will be delighted to see that many restaurants display no-smoking signs. However, this is seldom respected – the same places often have ashtrays on the tables.

Menu decoder

The vast majority of the menus you see in Goa will be in English, and it would be quite easy to get through the whole of your trip without uttering a word of any of the local dialects. However, any effort you make to do so – however faltering – will be appreciated. Also, if you're intending to go to some of the less touristy markets, English may not be spoken, so it's a good idea to know the local name for what you're after.

To call Goa's history chequered would be something of an understatement. The state has so many linguistic legacies and influences that English, Portuguese, Konkani, Hindi and Marathi are all spoken to some extent, not to mention Kannada, Gujarati and Urdu. For the sake of simplicity, the majority of the translation dishes and drinks below are described in Hindi, the national language of India.

INDIAN STAPLES

Chaat Salty snacks served with sweet and spicy chutneys

Chaval, chawu, bhat Rice

Dahi Yoghurt

Dudh Milk

Masko Butter

Naan Indian flat bread made from wheat and baked in a tandoor

Paan Betel leaf stuffed with supari (betel nut), quick lime paste, kathechu paste, gulukand (rose-petal preserve), fennel seeds and dried grated coconut, eaten after a meal to aid digestion. In big enough quantities it has a narcotic effect

Paneer Indian cottage cheese

Roti Bread

Sakor Sugar

Tatee, aanda Egg

Vindaloo Spicy curry, usually with pork

MAIN COURSES

Aadd maas Pork bones cooked in red spicy gravy

Ambot tik Sour and spicy fish or meat curry with tamarind

Assad roast Goan pork roast

Balchão Very spicy fish or pork dish in tomato sauce

Biryani Spiced saffron rice with pieces of lamb, chicken or vegetables

Cafreal Chicken marinated in green herb and garlic marinade and fried

Caldinha Meat or vegetables cooked in coconut milk, garlic, ginger and chillies

Chourico Spicy Portuguese smoked sausage

Fejoada Pungent gravy dish of sausage and dried beans

Isvon recheado Kingfish stuffed with chillies and spices in vinegar

Korma Mild curry, with chicken or vegetables, in coconut or yoghurt sauce

Sorpotel Spicy pork dish including the pig's organs

COOKING METHODS

Balti Indian wok or pot

Bhuna, **bhunao**, **jal frezi** Sautéed or stir-fried

Cafrial Marinated in hot sauce and dry-fried

Tandoor Traditional Indian clay oven

Xacuti Meat marinated in spicy coconut milk sauce and cooked until fairly dry

MEAT & FISH

Chaamp Chop

Gosht Lamb or beef

Jinga Prawns or shrimp

Khurzi Lamb or chicken, whole with spicy stuffing.

Macchi, **macchli** Fish

Murgh Chicken

Yakni Mutton

FRUIT & VEGETABLES

Aloo Potato

Am Mango

Brinjol Aubergine

Doroo Celery

Gajar Carrot

Gobhi, **gobi** Cauliflower

Kakadi Cucumber

Kela Banana

Matter, **mutter** Green peas

Naryal Coconut

Neem Curry leaf

Nimboo Lime

Papita Papaya

Phala, **phal** Fruit

Piaz, **peeaz**, **pyaz** Onion

Sabzi Generic term for vegetables

Tarbuz, **tarbuj** Watermelon

PULSES, NUTS & SEEDS

Channa Chickpea

Badam Almond

Dal, **dewa** Lentils or lentil soup
Kaju, **kajoo** Cashew nut
Meve Nuts
Palak, **saag**, **sag** Spinach or green leafy vegetable
Rai Mustard seed
Urid A type of lentil

SPICES & SEASONING
Adrak Ginger
Dalchini, **darchim** Cinnamon
Dhania Coriander
Elaichi Cardamom
Haldi, **huldi** Turmeric
Imli Tamarind
Jaifal, **taifal** Nutmeg
Javatri Mace
Jeera, **zeera** Cumin
Kokum Dried fruit which is used as a spice
Lasan Garlic
Lavang Cloves
Masala Spices, herbs and other seasonings ground or pounded together
Masala dabba Spice box containing the most popular dry spices
Mirch Pepper
Namak Salt
Tusci Basil
Zafron, **kesar** Saffron

DESSERTS
Bebinca Sweet coconut pancake dish put together one layer at a time
Dodol Thick, sweet and sticky Malaysian dessert with coconut milk, rice flour, jaggery and cashews
Kulkuls Fried dough snack often coated in syrup

DRINKS
Beer Beer
Chai Indian tea
Feni Traditional and powerful Goan drink made from cashews or coconut
Kofi Coffee
Lassi Tall cool drink of yoghurt and water made either sweet or salty
Sharab Wine
Udok, **pani** Water

AT THE RESTAURANT
Main shakahari hoon I'm a vegetarian
Bill de dijiyeh Bring the bill, please

Shopping

The standard advice for visitors to Goa is to go there with an empty suitcase, which you can then fill throughout your trip with various bargain buys. Shopping is a highlight, not only because what's on offer is such good value, but also because the state's markets – from the huge hippie bazaar at Anjuna to the hotchpotch collections of stalls that cluster around most tourist areas – are a cultural experience in themselves.

Shopping in Goa isn't entirely market based. As the state continually adapts to the influxes of foreign visitors and their tastes, some big-name Western clothes stores have sprung up, particularly in the towns frequented by the most tourists, such as the capital Panaji (try the MG Road and 18th June Road) and Calangute. Many of the higher profile brands manufacture their goods in the region, and so prices can be a fair bit lower than you'd expect to pay at home.

Visiting the state's markets – whether you're buying or not – gives all your five senses a blast of Goa. The best ones are alive with colourful products, and noisy with bargaining, begging and bagpipes. Vendors weave around the stalls peddling cakes, drinks and ice creams, all to a perpetual backdrop of competing music and incense sticks. Markets showcase Goa at its most vivid.

The state's most famous market – and a tourist attraction in its own right – is the Wednesday market at Anjuna. Shopping here is an intense experience, and on your arrival the immediate approach of beggars and pedlars can be rather overwhelming. But steel yourself and practise a firm 'no' and you'll soon get into the spirit of things: there are also plenty of places to stop for a breather and some refreshments when you're worn out. Saturday night bazaars in Arpora and Baga are less full on, and you'll have the advantage of being able to shop in the relative cool of the evening. As well as the main tourist ones, it's also worth checking out some of the markets used by Goans. You might not pick up any souvenirs there, but they give you a flavour of a more authentic way of life in the state, if you fancy getting off the tourist trail. And aside from the official markets, most places have a few stalls selling a motley collection of t-shirts, bags, sunglasses and similar.

With average wages across India low (many of the goods you will see on sale will come from outside Goa), almost everything on sale will seem a bargain. (The exception is imported goods, but they are not usually top of foreign visitors' shopping lists.) However, your obvious foreignness will work against you, and while few traders are out to con you as such, they naturally want to get as much as they can for what they sell. Whether you're at Anjuna market in full swing or at a lone street stall, it's almost always worth bargaining. The vendor knows that the cost of things in your home country is probably far higher than in Goa, and will fix his or her opening price accordingly. Follow the usual haggling rules. Ask around to find out what prices things usually go for, don't express too much eagerness over the particular item you want and make as if to

⬤ *Bag yourself a bargain at the local market*

walk away if the vendor won't come down far enough. However, do remember to keep things in perspective, and bear in mind that the amount you're negotiating over is probably just a pound or two, which will make very little difference to your holiday funds, but a lot of difference to an Indian trader.

If you're not a fan of bartering, some shops, particularly in the larger towns, do charge fixed, marked prices. This is less common at markets, although a few of the Western vendors, aware of some of their compatriots' discomfort with the bargaining culture, also use such a system. The posher stores selling foreign clothes will also have set prices.

Various souvenirs are on offer. Most prominent are clothes, such as holiday t-shirts and hats with Goa emblazoned across them, plus the hippie-chic range of flowing skirts, floaty tops and floppy hats. There's also an assortment of accessories, such as shoes, jewellery and bags, much of which – again – has a hippie theme. As you'd expect in India, textiles also feature quite prevalently, from small cushion covers to big bedspreads and everything in between, including material for clothesmaking if you prefer to do it yourself. Another option is to use the services of a tailor, which is fairly common practice in Goa, as across India. You won't be restricted to saris – many places will make Western business suits. Other staples include spices, incense sticks, CDs and general Indian bric-à-brac, as well as the standards that you might find in markets everywhere, such as sunglasses, cigarettes, lighters and wallets. Stalls in the coastal resorts usually also have a few inflatables, towels and flip-flops.

One word of warning: some taxi drivers will reduce your fare if you agree to visit a certain shop (which will reward the driver with a kickback). These places can often be very pleasant, air-conditioned and with professional, attentive service (serving plenty of cups of tea). The downside is that prices can be extortionate and you really get the hard sell, so leaving without buying anything can be somewhat awkward. If you don't like this kind of situation, it's worth refusing the driver's discount and avoiding the shop.

Children

Goa is massively popular with families. Golden beaches, reliable weather and low prices tempt parents to all the coastal resorts, while some of the northern beach towns are big draws for mums and dads of a hippie persuasion who want to introduce their outlandishly named offspring to their sub-culture. Family is central to Indian society, and most groups of local tourists will include at least one small child, so you will seldom feel out of place when travelling as a family. Goa is, if anything, even more child friendly than elsewhere in the country, and the laidback casualness of most of the restaurants and beach shacks is ideal when you have young kids in tow. Beach shacks are also well suited to watchful parents, allowing them to take a break with a drink while keeping an eye on the

⬤ *Coast plus children equals fun*

children as they play on the beach. However, if you are breastfeeding you should be sensitive to local attitudes: Indian women virtually never expose flesh – they even swim in the sea fully clothed – so exposing a breast, even to feed a child, is likely to be frowned upon. If you are determined to breastfeed in public, it's best to find a secluded spot.

The obvious entertainment for children is the beach. During the holiday season the sea is often calm enough even for weak swimmers, though of course you will want to look out for the flag system and note the presence or absence of a lifeguard. When they tire of scrabbling around in the sand and paddling, there are plenty of other beach-based activities. Boats go out from most of the busier resorts – the dolphin-spotting trips are a particular winner with children – and teenagers may well want to try some of the higher-octane pursuits like parasailing and jet-skiing, while younger family members can all get a lot of fun out of snorkelling. Hotels – particularly the more expensive ones – often have programmes of entertainment for children, and you may also find ad-hoc classes and activities at the resorts. Keep an eye out for posters advertising what's on, or ask other families.

Wildlife is another big attraction for young holidaymakers. There are several animal and bird sanctuaries in the state, the majority of which are inland. Elephant rides, which are on offer at some of the animal sanctuaries and at a handful of other tourist spots, usually go down well with children, and kids can also bathe elephants if sitting on top of one seems a bit too scary. Crocodile trips are also available for the more adventurous.

Sports & activities

Some visitors to Goa may want to do no more than lie on the beach, but if you do tire of sunbathing there are plenty of other options.

CULTURE

Renowned as it is for its pristine beaches and hedonistic party scene, it's sometimes easy to forget that Goa is part of a much larger country with a vast culture. Get away from the hotel strip and the beach and you will find curious little temples, gleaming white churches, centuries-old forts and museums, plus a rich heritage of art, architecture and music. It would be a shame to leave the state without having acquired a sense of its culture and history – along with the tan.

NATURE

There are several national parks, wildlife sanctuaries and protected areas in Goa, as well as some excellent bird-watching sites, particularly close to water and forests. You can find out more at
ⓦ www.goaforest.com

WATER SPORTS

The beach itself is the starting point for a lot of what's on offer. In the larger resorts – and sometimes even in the smaller ones too – there is a vast array of watersports catering for everyone from the laidback to adrenalin junkies. Jet-skiing, waterskiing, windsurfing, parasailing, scuba-diving, snorkelling, kite-surfing and kayaking are all tirelessly promoted by young men who roam the beaches, and you can also find more established operators with offices on or near the beach. The main watersport centres are Sinquerim, Calangute, Baga, Colva, and to some extent Benaulim, but even the smaller resorts usually offer a handful of activities. There are also boat trips available for fishing, dolphin spotting and sunset sails. In Panaji an entirely different kind of boat trip attracts tourists, who gamble on the city's floating casino or party on one of the booming disco boats. Away from the water, cricket and football are both hugely popular throughout Goa and, whether you intend to watch or play, you should find opportunities.

YOGA & AYURVEDA

If all this sounds rather exhausting, at the other end of the scale is the relaxing world of yoga, meditation and Ayurveda, the traditional Indian healing system. Treatments and classes are ubiquitous – you can even have an Ayurvedic massage on the beach in some places, although, as with anything, you get what you pay for. Yoga classes are particularly prevalent in the northern resorts that are more popular with hippies and backpackers, and tend to be advertised on notice boards around town and in cafés and restaurants. How much time you want to devote to it is up to you. If you're on a short trip or are just curious, pass an hour at a yoga class or 30 minutes treating yourself to a massage. Devotees meanwhile can spend weeks following a thorough programme that includes advice on eating the right foods alongside the exercise.

● *Transport yourself to yoga heaven*

Festivals & events

Both Hinduism and Christianity have played a vital part in shaping modern Goa, and the legacy is a plethora of different festivals. Unlike the majority of the Christian celebrations, which occur on set days, the Hindu festivities are based on the lunar calendar and so vary from year to year.

POP, BEAT AND JAZZ MUSIC FESTIVAL
Date varies, between February and May
A two-day music fest at Panaji's swish Kala Academy
📧 kalaacademy@kalaacademy.org 🅦 www.kalaacademy.org

SHIGMOTSAV
February to March
One of the main Hindu festivals, Shigmo, as it's also known, celebrates the end of winter. Running for a couple of weeks, it involves parades of

🔺 *Traditional dancers enliven festivals*

floats in Panaji, Margao, Mapusa, Vasco da Gama and Ponda, folk dancing and young people covering each other – and sometimes you – in brightly coloured flour and water.

CARNIVAL
Before Lent
Originally instituted by the Portuguese to celebrate the start of spring, Carnival has now widened its reach and welcomes people of every faith; many non-Goans also make the trip to attend. The revelry gets underway when the rotund character 'King Momo' decrees that everybody should have a good time. Celebrations include a colourful parade of floats, dancing, drinking, eating and general merrymaking. Carnival is one of the state's most popular festivals and if you fancy seeing it you need to book ahead.

PROCESSION OF ALL SAINTS
Fifth Monday of Lent
Starting from the Church of St Andrew, worshippers lug 30-plus statues on their shoulders around Old Goa and its neighbouring towns in the only event of this type to be held outside Rome. The piety of the day's procession gives way to more relaxed family fun in the evening.

BEACH BONANZA
From mid-April
Goans don't need religion as an excuse for a party. Beach Bonanza, which takes place on Sunday in Colva, is about nothing more than showing tourists a good time, with plenty of entertainment, drinking and dancing. The main action has now shifted from the beach to the village football ground.

 Postboxes are clearly marked

PRACTICAL INFORMATION

BOAT EXCURSIONS
CRUISE ON CHAPORA BACKWATER

LETTER

NO CLEARANCE ON
SUNDAYS &
HOLIDAYS
NEXT CLEARANCE
AT 11-30 &
15-00 HRS.
ANJUNA
403509

Preparing to go

GETTING THERE

By air

Current aviation regulations mean that if you take a scheduled flight from the UK and Europe to Goa you'll have to change planes, usually in Mumbai (Bombay), and sometimes in Delhi or Colombo in Sri Lanka. Several major airlines, including BA, SWISS, Austrian Airlines, Air France, Emirates and Sri Lankan Airlines link up with Jet Airways or Kingfisher to run flights from Europe with a stopover; Jet also operates out of London. From time to time airlines do offer discounts, but a scheduled flight is likely to set you back up to £500 in the high season.

A cheaper option can be to go on a charter flight, either with or without accommodation included, which also has the benefit of being direct, currently from Gatwick, Manchester and Birmingham. You should be able to get something for around £400, with further savings available if you book very far in advance or (sometimes) at the last minute. The law states that, whether you choose to come via a scheduled or charter flight, you must leave the same way. The journey time is around 11 hours.

If you're travelling from Ireland, you're likely to have to go via the UK. The US has direct flights to Mumbai, but it can be cheaper to come via Europe. Canadians can go via the US, Europe or Asia. From Australia, only Qantas flies non-stop to India, and leaving from New Zealand you will probably have to stopover in Asia.

Many people are aware that air travel emits CO_2, which contributes to climate change. You may be interested in the possibility of lessening the environmental impact of your flight through the charity Climate Care, which offsets your CO_2 by funding environmental projects around the world. Visit Ⓦ www.climatecare.org

By land

Driving to Goa from elsewhere in India is not recommended unless you're familiar with the conditions and have nerves of steel. Nor is hiring a car particularly cheap. But taxi and auto-rickshaw or tuk-tuk drivers are often prepared to make long journeys from one town to another, and cheap public trains and buses from nearby cities and states are also an option. In the case of buses, you are likely to have to pay a bit more for a ticket on a private bus, which will be more comfortable and probably air-conditioned.

TOURISM AUTHORITY

India has been keenly plugging itself as a tourist destination lately under the Incredible India slogan and has plenty of tourist offices around the world, including in London, Milan, Frankfurt, Paris, Amsterdam, New York, Los Angeles, Toronto, Sydney and Johannesburg. The full list of contact details is available at ⓦ www.incredibleindia.org

It's also worth taking a look at the Goa Tourist Department's site. If you have a specific question you can also give them a call.

ⓘ 0832 2438750/51/52 ⓦ www.goatourism.org

BEFORE YOU LEAVE

Doctors recommend that you are up to date with your hepatitis A, polio, typhoid, tetanus-diphtheria and MMR jabs for all travel to India. Inoculation against yellow fever is required if you've recently visited an infected area. Depending on the circumstances of your trip – whether you're visiting rural areas, interacting closely with local people or coming into contact with animals – rabies, hepatitis B and Japanese encephalitis injections may also be necessary. Anti-malarial medication is strongly

TRAVEL INSURANCE

Taking out travel insurance is strongly recommended and inexpensive. The most basic packages start from around £1 a day for a two-week or month-long break. For three months, expect to pay around £80. However, essential-cover-only packages exclude certain activities and, if you intend to ride a motorbike, scuba dive or similar, you may need to pay a bit more.

recommended. Consult your doctor at least a month before you go to ensure you have proper protection.

You should be able to buy pretty much anything you run out of on the trip. However, it can be worth taking a first-aid kit plus any medication with you.

ENTRY FORMALITIES

All foreign visitors to India require a visa and a passport valid for at least six months from your departure date. You can apply for a tourist visa in person or by post from the nearest Indian embassy, high commission or consulate general; the form is available online or you can pick one up in person. Unless there are any extenuating circumstances – if you have dual nationality or are applying from outside your country of residence, for example – the procedure is fairly simple and shouldn't take much more than a week. The fee is currently £30 for British nationals, and varies slightly from country to country. More information is available at
ⓦ www.hcilondon.net

You're permitted by customs laws to bring in 200 cigarettes (or 50 cigars or 250 g/9 oz of loose tobacco), a litre of spirits and 250 ml (8½ fl oz) of perfume. Expensive items such as video cameras technically ought to be declared on a Tourist Baggage Re-Export form, or you risk being charged duty on them when you leave India.

MONEY

The Indian currency is the rupee. In the main tourist resorts banks, ATMs and bureaux de change are easy to find, and accept pounds, euros and dollars. Your hotel may also change your money for you, but it's wise to check the rate first. Don't rely on your credit card outside Panaji – while some upmarket hotels and shops may take cards, the majority of low-budget accommodation, restaurants and cafés don't. It's worth planning ahead with your money if you're going off the beaten track. Try not to accept torn banknotes as you may have trouble getting rid of them.

CLIMATE

Goa's temperature stays hot throughout the year, averaging from 25 to 30°C (around 68 to 82°F). The holiday season runs roughly from October to March, with peak visiting time the two weeks over Christmas and New Year. This is a great time to visit for the party atmosphere, but you will pay for the privilege with higher prices and low availability. At either end of the season you can find great discounts and privacy, but you'll really feel the humidity in April and May, and by June the four-month monsoon season is kicking in, bringing heavy rains and rough seas. Few tourists choose to come at this time.

BAGGAGE ALLOWANCE

Baggage restrictions vary from one airline to another and, in the current political climate, from one month to the next. There's no substitute for checking your airline or operator's website in advance, giving them a call or checking with your travel agent. As a rule, scheduled airlines usually offer higher baggage allowances than chartered.

During your stay

AIRPORTS

Dabolim airport, the state's only one, is near Vasco da Gama and around 30 km (19 miles) from the capital Panaji. There's a pre-paid taxi booth just outside, which displays the costs to certain destinations. You'll be besieged by taxi drivers as soon as you emerge. You should be able to bargain one down to a decent fare. Otherwise, turn left when you leave the airport and walk up the hill, where you can pick up buses to Vasco da Gama and continue your journey via another bus or on the train.

Bear in mind that the airport can be bureaucratic and chaotic, so on your way home it can be worth turning up more than the suggested two hours in advance.

☎ 0832 2513806 ☎ 0832 2501630

COMMUNICATIONS

There are plenty of places from which you can make phone calls: look for the signs that read STD/ISD/PCO in small shops and kiosks. Some have coin-operated payphones; at others the call is metered and you pay at the end. Expect to pay up to 40 rupees a minute. Internet cafés are increasingly offering phone calls, which can work out a lot cheaper. There's good mobile reception in most areas. If you're staying for a while, you could buy a local SIM card (you'll need your passport).

Goa's postal service is reliable but slow, with letters sent overseas taking anything up to three weeks to arrive. You should pay less than 10 rupees to send a postcard abroad, a letter may cost about double that. As well as at post offices, stamps are sometimes on sale along with postcards. Some hotels will also mail cards for you.

Postboxes are rectangular and red, and fairly easy to spot.

CUSTOMS

Watch out for the Indian side-to-side head movement in response to questions. Whether this means yes, no, maybe or I don't know depends on the circumstances. If you need to extract crucial information, try to get a verbal answer.

DRESS CODES

While Goa is laid back and fully geared up for tourists, it's still part of a very traditional country. Topless and nude sunbathing are against the law; while that is unlikely to be enforced, stripping off can still offend local sensibilities. Some restraint is appreciated. If you do decide to bare all, the hippie beaches of Anjuna, Arambol and relaxed Vagator are probably the best places to go to.

In religious buildings, more modest dress is required. If you're visiting a temple, you should take off your shoes at the entrance, and it's good manners to offer to do so if going into an Indian person's home, although they may well tell you not to bother.

TELEPHONING GOA

From Europe 00 + 91 + 832 + number
From the US & Canada 011 + 91 + 832 + number
From Australia 0011 + 91 + 832 + number
From New Zealand 00 + 91 + 832 + number
From South Africa 00 + 91 + 832 + number

TELEPHONING ABROAD

UK 00 + 44 + number
US & Canada 00 + 1 + number
Australia 00 + 61 + number
New Zealand 00 + 64 + number
South Africa 00 + 27 + number

To get a telephone number, dial 191 or 197 for Directory Enquiries. 195 is the number for assistance with numbers that have changed. To get the operator, call 199.

ELECTRICITY

Goa's current is 230 to 240 volts/50 Hz. The plug socket is three round
pins, but comes in two sizes. European appliances usually fit loosely into
the smaller kind, but you may need to wedge the plug in place. Cheap
adaptors are easy to find. However, power cuts are common.

EMERGENCIES

EMERGENCY NUMBERS
Ambulance 102
Fire 101
Police 100, 0832 2428482 (North Goa), 0832 2705094 (South Goa)
Tourist Police 0832 2437038
Coastguard 0832 2531718, 0832 2520584

Medical facilities in Goa may seem on the primitive side to the Western
patient. The best ones are based in the larger towns; fortunately, given
the size of the state, you should never be too far away from somewhere
with decent amenities. If you need medical treatment, the best thing is
to ask at your hotel; many of them have a doctor on call and, even if they
don't, they are likely to be able to point you in the right direction. Almost
all doctors in Goa speak English. If you're out, a cab driver should know
the nearest place. In an emergency, bear in mind that calling an
ambulance can be slow and your best bet may be to take a taxi.

Goa Medical College ⓐ Dayanand Bandodkar Marg ❶ 0832 2458700
Goa Medical College Hospital ⓐ Bambolim, NH 17, 9 km (5½ miles) south
of Panaji ❶ 0832 2458700, 0832 2233700 ❶ 0832 2458727
ⓔ goamed@hotmail.com
Mapusa Clinic ⓐ Mapusa Clinic Road, Mapusa ❶ 0832 2262350
ⓦ www.mapusaclinic.com (currently under construction)
Margao Main Hospital ⓐ Padre Miranda Road ❶ 0832 2705664

There are no embassies in Goa itself.

British Deputy High Commission ⓐ Maker Chambers IV, 2nd Floor, 222 Jamnalal Bajaj Road, Nariman Point, Mumbai ⓣ 022 56502222 ⓕ 022 22027940

British Tourist Assistance Office in Goa ⓐ S-13/14 Dempo Towers, Patto Plaza, Panaji ⓣ 0832 2438897 ⓔ bcagoa@sancharnet.in

Irish Embassy ⓐ 230 Jor Bagh, New Delhi 3 ⓣ 011 24626733 ⓕ 011 24603335 ⓦ www.irelandinindia.com ⓛ 09.00–12.30, 14.30–17.00

U.S. Consulate General ⓐ Lincoln House, 78 Bhulabhai Desai Road, Mumbai ⓣ 022 23633611 ⓦ http://mumbai.usconsulate.gov

Australia Consulate General ⓐ 3rd Floor, 36 Maker Chambers VI, 220 Nariman Point, Mumbai ⓣ 022 56692000 ⓦ www.india.embassy.gov.au

New Zealand High Commission ⓐ Sir Edmund Hillary Marg, Chanakyapuri, New Delhi ⓣ 011 26883170 ⓕ 011 26883165 ⓦ www.nzembassy.com ⓛ 08.30–17.00 hrs Mon–Fri.

South African High Commission ⓐ B-18, Vasant Marg, New Delhi ⓣ 011 614941120 ⓕ 011 6143605 ⓔ tourism@sahc-india.com ⓦ www.sahc-india.com

The 24-hour helpline ⓣ 0832 2412121 has information on everything from medical care to restaurants.

GETTING AROUND
Car hire
Because of India's chaotic driving conditions, few tourists opt to hire a car. It's usually much easier and cheaper to get the car with the driver, which can be done either through a travel agent or hotel, or just by negotiating with a taxi driver. A day's worth of travelling shouldn't set you back any more than 1,000 rupees. If you're not coming back to the starting point, clarify whether the driver's return journey is included.

If you do intend to drive yourself, it's a good idea to bring an international licence with you. Traffic in the cities can be a nightmare of hold-ups and hooting. In the country, roads are usually uneven and there aren't many signs or streetlights. Indians drive on the left.

Motorbike & bicycle hire

A motorbike is perfect for zipping around to remote beaches. You can hire anything from a scooter up to an Enfield. This can be done through your hotel, a travel agent or on the street. Although few tourists seem to bother, wearing a helmet is required by law and is also a good idea, given India's appalling road-safety statistics. If you're not going that far, renting a bicycle (or even buying one, if you're staying a while) is another option.

Public transport

Taking a bus in Goa is not only ridiculously cheap, but also a fun way to see some of the local life. Buses don't tend to go along the coast; you'll probably need to come inland and change. The main hubs are Mapusa, Panaji and Margao. You normally pay the conductor on board. Some private buses offer more comfort for a higher fare.

The state has two main railway lines, one running north–south and the other east–west. Few of the stations are well placed for the beach resorts, though. Train enquiry line (Margao Station): ☎ 0832 2712790.

HEALTH, SAFETY & CRIME

As in the rest of India, take care with what you eat and drink. Mindful of the importance of their reputations, the vast majority of Goa's hotels, restaurants and beach shacks maintain high standards of hygiene and use bottled water for ice. Check the seals on bottled water to ensure they have not been refilled with tap water. Healthcare in Goa is not expensive, but the standards are lower than you might be used to. The most reliable hospitals are listed in the Emergencies section.

Goa generally feels safe, but the preponderance of 'rich' tourists in a very poor country does have its inherent risks. Violent crimes, such as muggings, are unusual but do occur. Take care to secure your possessions, whether they are in the hotel, on your person or on the beach while you're swimming. Be discreet with your valuables, and pay close attention in crowded places. Women travellers in particular should avoid walking alone at night in lonely areas. Be particularly wary about accepting food or drink from strangers, as drugging incidents, though rare, have been reported. Anything involving export licences or money changing should set your alarm bells ringing.

The state also presents a few low-level hassles, such as taxi drivers who want to take you to shops or hotels that give them commission, but these can usually be dealt with by a firm refusal.

MEDIA

It's easy to find English media in Goa. There are three English-language newspapers, *The Navhind Times*, *The Herald* and *The Gomantak Times*, plus the weekly *Goan Observer* and monthly magazine *Goa Today*. Your hotel is likely to have the usual selection of cable channels – BBC World, CNN, MTV, HBO, the Discovery Channel and so on. Some local Indian channels, both television and radio, also broadcast in English.

OPENING HOURS

Many shops catering to tourists start the day early and stay open as long as holidaymakers are up and about. Most restaurants and beach shacks open around 07.00 or 08.00 and serve food until at least 23.00, sometimes later. Banks tend to operate from 10.00 to 14.00 from Monday to Friday, and from 10.00 to 12.00 on Saturday, although some stay open later, especially in larger towns. Bureaux de change often stay open until the early evening or later. Religious buildings keep differing hours, but temples frequently open from very early in the morning. Businesses often close for a siesta, from 12.00 or 13.00 to 15.00 or 15.30.

RELIGION

Almost two thirds of Goans are Hindu and around one third Christian – a legacy of Portuguese rule; a minority are Muslim. Goans are generally tolerant of other people's faiths.

TIME DIFFERENCES

Goa is 5.5 hours ahead of GMT, 4.5 ahead of most of mainland Europe. It is 10.5 ahead of EST and 13.5 ahead of PST, 5.5 hours behind Sydney and 7.5 behind Auckland.

TIPPING

It's customary to tip in restaurants and in your hotel. Tipping 10 per cent of your bill when eating out is the norm; in hotels 10 or 20 rupees should suffice. There's no need to tip a taxi driver who takes you a short distance, but if you've hired the driver for the day he will probably expect a little extra.

TOILETS

The majority of conveniences you encounter will be Western style. All restaurants and beach shacks have their own toilets or access to one, which are usually clean enough. It's best to carry around some tissues as an emergency loo-roll stash; Indians don't use toilet paper.

TRAVELLERS WITH DISABILITIES

Goa is not the easiest place to get around if you have impaired mobility. The pavements – where there are any – can be narrow and uneven, and few facilities outside the top hotels have wheelchair access. But Goans are usually helpful and accommodating where they can be, and the low costs mean that staying in adapted accommodation and travelling with a car and a driver should be affordable.

The following organisations offer various degrees of advice to travellers with disabilities:

The Royal Association for Disability and Rehabilitation does not offer an advice service for individuals, but its website has a news bulletin board on which the editor posts details of overseas travel services. ⓐ 12 City Forum, 250 City Road, London EC1V 8AF ⓣ 020 7250 3222 ⓕ 020 7250 0212 ⓔ radar@radar.org.uk ⓦ www.radar.org.uk

Tourism for All ⓐ The Hawkins Suite, Enham Place, Enham Alamein, Andover SP11 6JS ⓣ 0845 124 9971 ⓕ 0845 124 9972 ⓔ info@tourismforall.org.uk

Disability Goa ⓐ Star Investments, Opp. Head Post Office, Panjim, Goa ⓣ 0832 2427160 ⓔ dragoa@rediffmail.com ⓦ www.disabilitygoa.com

A

air travel 114, 118
Anjuna 25–9
Arambol 14–19
architecture 53, 76, 83
art galleries
    Bom Jesus Basilica Art Gallery
        83–4
    Kerkar Art Complex 40
    Kristu Kala Mandir Art Gallery 85
Art Park Campal 54
Ayurveda 39, 50–1, 62, 71–2, 110

B

Baga 31–5
baggage allowance 117
Bardez taluka 76–7
beaches 14, 20–1, 25, 31, 37–9, 44,
    48–9, 53–4, 61–2, 66, 70, 107–8,
    109
Benaulim 66–9
bird-watching 81–2
boats 40–1, 45–6, 48–9, 53, 68, 81, 109
buses 83, 115, 122

C

Calangute 37–43
Candolim 44–7
casino 58–9
cathedral 86
children 107–8
churches
    Basilica of Bom Jesus 83–4
    Church of Our Lady of the
        Immaculate Conception 54
    Church of Our Lady of Mercy 62
    Church of St Francis of Assisi 84
climate 117
Colva 61–5
communication 118–19
consulates 121
crime 122–3
customs and duty 116

D

disabilities, travellers with 124
dolphin-watching 49, 61–2
Dona Paula Beach 53
Dr Salim Ali Bird Sanctuary
    81–2
dress 119
driving 114, 121

E

electricity 120
elephants 108
emergencies 120–1
etiquette 108, 119
excursions 40–1, 45–6, 55–6,
    76–94

F

family 107–8
ferries 81
festivals 111–12
fishing 61
food and drink 96–103
    fruit 98–9
    menus 101–3
    places to eat 16–19, 21–3, 27–9,
        33–5, 41–3, 44, 46–7, 51, 57–8, 62,
        64–5, 68–9, 72–4, 76–7, 80, 82,
        86, 89, 93–4, 100
    rice 98
    seafood 69, 93, 96
    tea 98
Fort Aguada 78–80

G

gardens 54, 93

H

health 115–16, 120, 122
hippies 8, 14, 25, 106

I

insurance 115

K
Kala Academy 59

M
Mandovi River 53
Margao 91–4
massage 50–1, 110
media 123
meditation 16, 45
Miramar 53
money 116
motorbikes 122
Municipal Gardens 93
museums
    Archaeology Museum 83
    Goa State Museum 54
    Houses of Goa Museum 76

N
nightlife 18–19, 22–3, 28–9, 31, 33–5, 41–3, 46–7, 51, 57–9, 62, 64–5, 69, 72–4, 77, 94

O
Old Goa 83–6
opening hours 123

P
Palolem 70–4
Panaji 53–9
passports and visas 116
phones 118, 119
Ponda 87–9
post 118

R
religion 111–12, 123

S
safety 122–3
scuba diving 33
shopping 61, 67, 104–6
    bargaining 105–6

    food and drink 93
    markets 20, 25–6, 33, 39, 66, 91, 93, 104–5
    souvenirs 26, 106
    textiles 106
Sinquerim 48–51
smoking 100
spice farms 87
swimming 53–4

T
Tai Chi 16
taxis 106, 120, 121
temples 88–9
    Damodar Temple 93
    Maruti Temple 54–5
    Shantadurga Temple 89
    Shri Mahalsa 89
    Sri Manguesh Temple 89
time differences 123
tipping 124
toilets 124
tourist information 115, 121, 124
trains 122
TV 123

V
Vagator 20–3

W
watersports 14–16, 31, 33, 40, 49, 51, 53–4, 61–2, 67–8, 70, 108, 109
wildlife sanctuaries 81–2, 108

Y
yoga 16, 27, 39, 45, 71, 110

ACKNOWLEDGEMENTS

The publishers would like to thank the following individuals and organisations for providing their copyright photographs for this book:

World Pictures/Photoshot pages 13, 15, 21, 23, 26, 27, 32, 38, 45, 49, 63, 68, 71, 77, 79, 82, 95, 105, 107
Pictures Colour Library pages 5, 10, 28, 97, 99
All the rest, Vasile Szakacs

Copy editor: Penny Isaac
Proofreader: Ian Faulkner

Send your thoughts to
books@thomascook.com

- Found a beach bar, peaceful stretch of sand or must-see sight that we don't feature?
- Like to tip us off about any information that needs a little updating?
- Want to tell us what you love about this handy little guidebook and more importantly how we can make it even handier?

Then here's your chance to tell all! Send us ideas, discoveries and recommendations today and then look out for your valuable input in the next edition of this title.

Send an email to the above address or write to:
HotSpots Project Editor, Thomas Cook Publishing, PO Box 227, Coningsby Road, Peterborough PE3 8SB, UK